LEGENDS OF WARFARE

NAVAL

USS New Jersey (BB-62)

From World War II, Korea, and Vietnam to Museum Ship

DAVID DOYLE

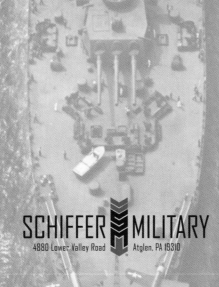

SCHIFFER MILITARY

4880 Lower Valley Road   Atglen, PA 19310

Designed by Justin Watkinson
Type set in Impact/Minion Pro/Univers LT Std

ISBN: 978-0-7643-5663-6
Printed in China

Published by Schiffer Publishing, Ltd.
4880 Lower Valley Road
Atglen, PA 19310
Phone: (610) 593-1777; Fax: (610) 593-2002
E-mail: Info@schifferbooks.com
www.schifferbooks.com

For our complete selection of fine books on this and related subjects, please visit our website at www.schifferbooks.com. You may also write for a free catalog.

Schiffer Publishing's titles are available at special discounts for bulk purchases for sales promotions or premiums. Special editions, including personalized covers, corporate imprints, and excerpts, can be created in large quantities for special needs. For more information, contact the publisher.

We are always looking for people to write books on new and related subjects. If you have an idea for a book, please contact us at proposals@schifferbooks.com.

Acknowledgments

This book would not have been possible without the gracious help of many individuals and institutions. Among my many friends who contributed invaluable help in completing this book are Tom Kailbourn, Scott Taylor, Dana Bell, Dave Baker, Tracy White, Rick Davis, Roger Torgeson, Sean Hert, and James Noblin. Their generous and skillful assistance adds immensely to the quality of this volume. Additionally, the very professional and helpful staff on the National Archives and the Navy Museum went out of their way to assist with the project. Finally, beyond having the help of such wonderful friends and colleagues, the Lord has blessed me with a wonderful wife, Denise, who has tirelessly scanned thousands of photos and documents for this and numerous other books. More importantly, she consistently provided encouragement when this project seemed stagnated by various obstacles, and is an ongoing source of joy.

Contents

Introduction

"Firepower for Freedom" was the motto of USS *New Jersey*, and it was fitting indeed. *New Jersey* plied the seas, using its guns and sometimes its mere presence to counter tyranny, aggression, and communism around the world over a fifty-year-plus span. Its massive 16-inch guns, each capable of hurling 1-ton shells over 20-plus miles around the clock, were immune to rain and darkness and, once the triggers were pulled, were immune too to any type of electronic countermeasures.

New Jersey was the second of six *Iowa*-class battleships authorized, and the second built of the four actually completed.

Its heavy armor plate—over 17 inches thick in places, far heavier than any produced for decades—provided more than adequate protection against most weapons through the many decades of service. When President Ronald Reagan ordered all four *Iowa*s reactivated in the 1980s, a news crew aboard one of the vessels asked the captain what the effect would be of an Exocet missile, which had gained fame in the Falklands, on the battleship. His response was that it would be about the same as when a kamikaze had struck an *Iowa* decades before—push the debris over the side, touch up the paint, and keep going!

While it is true that no ship is invulnerable to attack—and that includes *New Jersey* and the rest of the *Iowa* class ships—their heavy construction meant that only a few nations possessed weapons potent enough to be a real threat; this was an important consideration when operating off Korea, Vietnam, Lebanon, and Iraq.

USS *New Jersey* Data	
Builder	Philadelphia Navy Yard
Laid Down	September 16, 1940
Launched	December 7, 1942
Commissioned	May 23, 1943
Decommissioned	June 30, 1948
Recommissioned	November 21, 1950
Decommissioned	August 21, 1957
Recommissioned	April 6, 1968
Decommissioned	December 17, 1969
Recommissioned	December 28, 1982
Decommissioned	September 9, 1991
Struck	January 12, 1995
Reinstated	February 12, 1998
Stricken for preservation	January 4, 1999
Class	*Iowa*
Sponsor	Mrs. Carolyn Edison
Displacement, standard	45,000 tons
Displacement, full load 1945	57,540 tons
Displacement, full load 1988	57,500 tons
Length, waterline, full load	860'
Length, overall	887' 6⅝"
Beam, maximum	108' 1⅜"
Draft at full-load displacement	38'
Bunker fuel	8,624 tons (1945)
Endurance (design)	14,890 nautical miles @ 15 knots
Boilers	8 Babcock and Wilcox, 565 psi
Machinery	4 Westinghouse geared turbines, 212,000 total shaft horsepower
Speed	33 knots
Armor	13.5" belt; 5" on 50 lbs., armor deck; 60 lbs. bomb deck; 11.2" bulkheads; 17.3" conning tower; 17.3" barbettes; 17" gunhouses
Armament, June 1944	9 16"/50 in three triple turrets, 10 dual 5"/38 gun mounts; 16 quad 40 mm mounts; 49 20 mm single mounts
Armament, May 1986	9 16"/50 in three triple turrets, 6 dual 5"/38 gun mounts; 32 BGM-109 Tomahawk; 16 RGM-84 Harpoon; 4 20 mm CWIS
Crew 1945	189 officers, 2,789 enlisted
Crew 1988	65 officers, 1,445 enlisted

CHAPTER 1
Construction

A little over two weeks after the keel-laying ceremony, this was the state of construction on the *New Jersey*, on October 3, 1940. The view is from the port side of the stern, facing forward. Two layers of plate floors (lateral frame members with lightening holes) are being assembled along the centerline, the bottom tier resting on the shell plating, the outer skin of the hull. The area shown in the photo will be built out from the centerline to receive a triple bottom, consisting of steel plating on the bottom, in between the lower and upper plate floor members, and atop the upper frame members. This will provide extra protection for the bottom of the hull as well as spaces for storing diesel oil, fuel oil, fresh water, and feed water. *National Archives*

USS *New Jersey*, BB-62, was the second of six *Iowa*-class fast battleships authorized for construction by Congress. The *Iowa*-class ships were the final battleships built for the US Navy and represented the zenith of design for fast, heavily armed, and heavily armored combatants. Construction of the *New Jersey* began at the Philadelphia Navy Yard on September 16, 1940. The same yard also built USS *Wisconsin* (BB-64) and the fifth *Iowa*-class battleship, BB-65, the *Illinois*, construction of which was canceled in August 1945 when it was 22 percent complete.

In order to accommodate the hull of the massive battleships, the builder's ways at the shipyard had to be enlarged. Shipways 2 and 3 each were lengthened by 325 feet, to 1,135 feet each, allowing *New Jersey* and *Wisconsin* to be built side by side, almost simultaneously (construction on *Wisconsin* began in January 1941).

Unlike most prior battleships, the heavy armor plates forming the side belt armor were mounted internally, meaning that they had to be installed while the ship was on the ways. Likewise, the turbines and machinery were installed while on the ways, leading to a launching weight of 36,446 tons—one of the heaviest launching weights in the world—but still only a portion of its ultimate total weight.

U.S.S. NEW JERSEY.
AFT LOOKING FORWARD.
NAVY YARD, PHILA., PA.
JAN. 9-1941
73-41-B.

By the time this view from above the stern, looking forward, was taken on January 9, 1941, work on the triple bottom was still ongoing in the foreground, but in the background, a huge, transverse bulkhead, part of the citadel—the internal armored protection for the vital machinery and systems in the center of the hull—was under construction at the forward end of the soon-to-be machinery spaces. *National Archives*

A July 15, 1941, view of the *New Jersey* taken above the bow shows that in the six months since the preceding photo was taken, the barbettes for turrets 1 and 2 were well advanced in construction. The barbettes were heavily armored cylinders that would contain machinery and ammunition-handling and storing facilities for the turrets. Before the turrets were installed, the gabled shelters seen here often were laid atop the barbettes to keep the elements out. Staging had been erected around the ship for the shipwrights to work from while building up the sides of the hull. *National Archives*

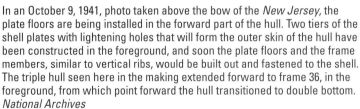

In an October 9, 1941, photo taken above the bow of the *New Jersey*, the plate floors are being installed in the forward part of the hull. Two tiers of the shell plates with lightening holes that will form the outer skin of the hull have been constructed in the foreground, and soon the plate floors and the frame members, similar to vertical ribs, would be built out and fastened to the shell. The triple hull seen here in the making extended forward to frame 36, in the foreground, from which point forward the hull transitioned to double bottom. *National Archives*

Another October 9, 1941, elevated photo of the *New Jersey* shows the progress of construction from above the stern forward. In the foreground is the barbette for turret 3, with a shelter made of canvas over a frame positioned atop it. Cables are attached to the shelter, for lifting it off the barbette when necessary. Many lateral and fore-and-aft bulkheads and several levels of decks have been constructed between the barbettes for turret 3 and, in the background, turret 2. *National Archives*

The forecastle is receiving its steel plating in this view from above the bow on July 8, 1942, five months before the ship's launching. Farther aft, from frames 50 to 166, the main deck, of which the forecastle is part, was covered with 1.5-inch STS (special-treatment steel) armor. This part of the main deck was referred to as the bomb deck and was intended to detonate bombs and projectiles before they could penetrate that deck. If bombs or projectiles did pass through the bomb deck, the 2nd deck—the armor deck—was designed to protect the vital interior of the hull. *National Archives*

In an undated photograph apparently taken on or near the same date as the preceding one, judging by the progress on the forecastle in the background, the shelters have been removed from the tops of the barbettes for turrets 1 and 2. The impressive thickness of the armor of the barbette for turret 2 (the closer barbette) is apparent. The barbette was constructed of Class A armor, ranging in thickness from 17.3 inches to 11.6 inches. *National Archives*

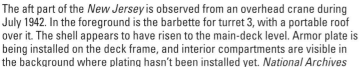

The aft part of the *New Jersey* is observed from an overhead crane during July 1942. In the foreground is the barbette for turret 3, with a portable roof over it. The shell appears to have risen to the main-deck level. Armor plate is being installed on the deck frame, and interior compartments are visible in the background where plating hasn't been installed yet. *National Archives*

Almost twenty-seven months after the keel of the battleship *New Jersey* was laid, the ship was launched at the Philadelphia Naval Shipyard, on the first anniversary of the Japanese attack on Pearl Harbor: December 7, 1942. Here, the *New Jersey* is poised on its building ways on that date, prior to the arrival of the dignitaries and spectators who will attend the launching ceremony. In front of the bulbous bow is the stand for the christening party. Hanging from the bow are the two anchors and their chains. Attached with cables to the lower part of the bow are the fore poppets, which helped support the weight of the ship on the ways. *National Archives*

The *New Jersey* is viewed from a higher perspective on December 7, 1942, before the launching ceremony. In the hours leading up to the launching, workers executed a carefully choreographed sequence of steps to transfer the massive weight of the ship from the keel and bilge blocks, upon which it was built, to the launching cradle. This involved knocking out the shoring and the blocks one by one. Note the conical shelters over the barbettes for turrets 1 and 2, to the rear of which are the conning tower and the partially constructed superstructure. *National Archives*

A better view is available in this launching-day photo of the starboard side of the fore poppets. The poppets were carefully constructed to adhere tightly to the contours of the hull. Cables held them in place until after the launching, when the poppets were removed. The poppets formed a sort of cradle, to support and stabilize the ship as it slid down the ways and into the water upon launching. Painted in white on the bow are draft marks, for establishing the depth of the hull in the water, and grid lines, apparently for photo-reference purposes during the launching of the ship. *National Archives*

The *New Jersey* is observed off its starboard stern on launching day, December 7, 1942. Towering above the ship is the overhead crane, with its numerous support towers. "NEW JERSEY" is lettered on the stern, which was not supported by poppets; the structural strength of the stern had to suffice to support it, cantilevered over the water such as it was. *National Archives*

As seen in a closer view of the starboard stern on launching day, the four propellers and the two rudders were not mounted until after the ship was launched. The rudder posts are on either side of the centerline; farther outboard are the propeller shafts. The two inboard propeller shafts are housed in skegs, while the two outboard propeller shafts are supported by struts. The starboard aft poppet is between the inboard and the outboard starboard propeller shafts. Numerous workmen, dwarfed by the ship, are on the ways, going about the work of preparing the ship for launching. *National Archives*

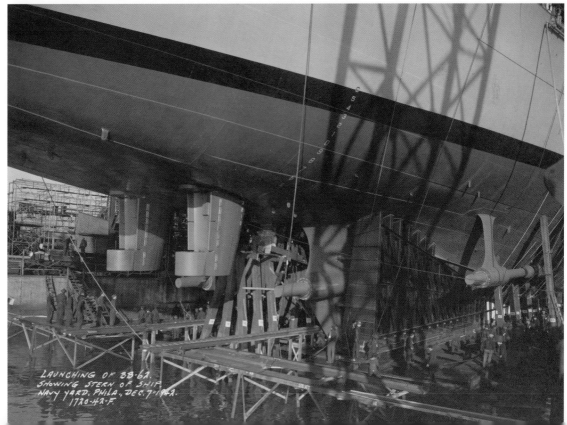

CHAPTER 2
Launching, Fitting Out, and World War II Service

New Jersey was launched on the first anniversary of the Pearl Harbor attack—December 7, 1942. The ship's sponsor, smashing the bottle of champagne over the bow and christening the ship *New Jersey*, was Carolyn Edison, wife of Charles Edison—he was a son of inventor Thomas Edison and secretary of the US Navy.

At the appointed time, the *New Jersey* slid down the ways into the Delaware River, slewing cables coupling the hull to mounds of anchor chain in an effort to haul the hull of *New Jersey* into a position parallel with the course of the river during the launching. This did not go exactly as planned, and instead the stern of the battleship briefly visited its namesake state. Tugboats quickly rectified this error, and the hull was moved to a dry dock for removal of launching equipment and the machining of the turret roller paths. From there it was moved to Pier 4 for fitting out.

The fitting-out complete, at 1238 on May 23, 1943, USS *New Jersey* was placed in commission. The ship and crew immediately began a training and shakedown period in the Western Atlantic and Caribbean before being sent to the Pacific. The ship passed through the Panama Canal on January 7, 1944.

In the Pacific it joined Task Group 58.2, a unit of the US 5th Fleet, and on February 4, 1944, became the flagship of Adm. Raymond Spruance, commander of the 5th Fleet. During action against Truk, *New Jersey*'s 5-inch secondary battery engaged a Japanese trawler on February 16, sinking the enemy ship. At a range of 32,200 yards, *New Jersey*'s main battery fired on a Japanese destroyer, the *Nowaki*, but the Japanese ship was able to take evasive action and avoid being hit.

On April 30, *New Jersey* joined *Iowa*, *Alabama*, *Indiana*, *Massachusetts*, *North Carolina*, and *South Dakota* in bombarding Ponape.

Putting into Pearl Harbor on August 24, Adm. William Halsey broke his flag on *New Jersey*, making it the flagship of the Third Fleet. *New Jersey* would spend the next eight months operating out of Ulithi. In October, while screening carriers headed toward Luzon, *New Jersey*'s antiaircraft gunners downed a Japanese airplane, which crashed into the carrier *Intrepid*. *Intrepid*'s own gunners, firing at the enemy, accidentally shot and wounded three of *New Jersey*'s men.

Mother Nature put *New Jersey* and the rest of Task Force 38 to the test on December 18, when the task force was engulfed by Typhoon Cobra. While three destroyers were sunk, three more were seriously damaged, as was a cruiser, and five aircraft carriers were damaged (and 146 aircraft were destroyed), with 790 men lost from these vessels. But for a bent propeller shaft on *Iowa*, *New Jersey* and the other seven battleships of Task Force 38 suffered only modest damage.

On January 25, 1945, Halsey transferred his flag from *New Jersey*, but two days later it became the flagship of RAdm. Oscar Badger, commander of Battleship Division 7. In February, it screened carriers off Iwo Jima, and the following month did the same off Okinawa, where it also used its guns for bombardment on the twenty-fourth. On Easter Sunday, April 1, the destroyer *Franks* darted in front of the *New Jersey* while both vessels were escorting *Yorktown*. Quick action by *New Jersey*'s officer of the deck, Lt. Gene Hayward, prevented the battleship from running down the destroyer entirely, although the ships did sideswipe each other, port to port. The battleship was minimally damaged, but the destroyer, while afloat, was badly damaged and its captain was mortally wounded by the collision.

Following a May–July overhaul at Puget Sound, during which time a new, larger bridge was installed, *New Jersey* returned to Japanese waters in August, again becoming flagship of the 5th Fleet. *New Jersey* steamed into Tokyo Bay on September 17, where it served as flagship until January 28.

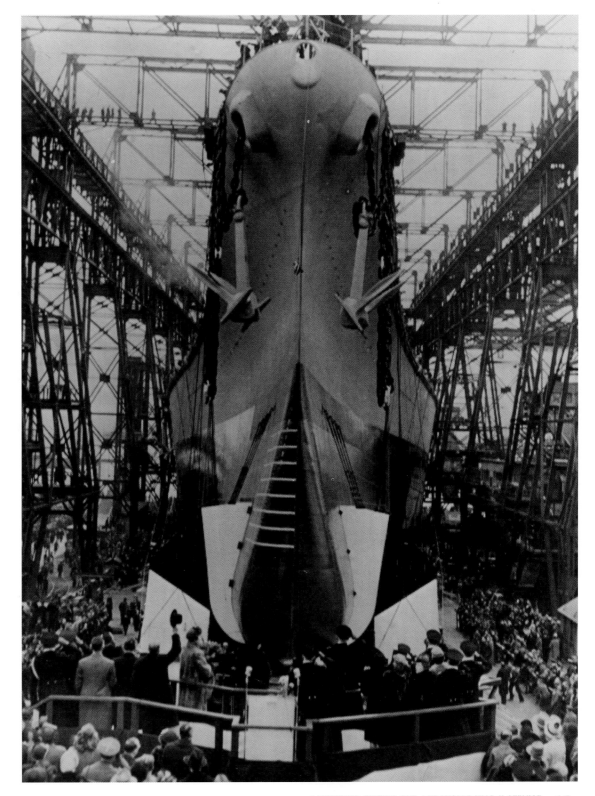

Later on launching day, a large crowd has gathered along the *New Jersey* and on the overhead crane, and dignitaries are on the platform, preparing to christen the ship. *Naval History and Heritage Command*

The sponsor of the battleship *New Jersey*, Carolyn Hawkins Edison, prepares to smash the ceremonial bottle of champagne on the bow of the ship. Mrs. Edison was the wife of Charles Edison, a son of the inventor Thomas Alva Edison. Then-recently secretary of the Navy under President Franklin Delano Roosevelt, Charles Edison was governor of New Jersey by the time of the launching.

After the *New Jersey* was christened with champagne, a series of triggers were actuated by hydraulic power, releasing the tethers holding the ship in place. Gravity then took over, and the ship began its slide rearward down the ways and into the Delaware River. In a view of the ship as it draws away from the christening stand, the fore poppets are moving down the twin main ground ways. For a ship of this size, it also was necessary to use two narrower ground ways outboard of the main ones, and the port outboard ground way may be seen here, supporting the wide part of the hull amidships. *Naval History and Heritage Command*

Gathering momentum, the ship slides down the ways, with most of the bottom of the hull now in the water. Spectators have begun to step onto the ways, for a better view of the massive hull as it becomes waterborne. Once the stern entered the water and began to lift, the fore poppet suddenly bore much more of the weight of the ship: up to twenty-five percent of it. Thus, it was essential to make the fore poppet very strong.

On the christening platform, VIPs wave as the *New Jersey* enters the Delaware River during its launching on December 7, 1942. The basic structures of the superstructure are present, including the heavily armored conning tower at the front, followed by the forward superstructure, the two smokestacks, and the tapered tower for the aft main-battery director. Three of the five twin 5-inch/38-caliber dual-purpose gun mounts are present alongside the superstructure. *Maritime Quest*

The *New Jersey* is viewed from the starboard side as the hull enters the Delaware River upon launching. *National Archives*

The *New Jersey* is fully waterborne. During the launching, three anchor chains originally were to have been attached to the starboard side of the hull, to cause it to turn as its momentum carried it into the river, in order to avoid becoming grounded on the New Jersey side of the river. However, one of the chains was omitted intentionally during the preparations for launching, and upon launching the two remaining chains did not sufficiently control the course of the ship. This resulted in the ship coming too close to shore and damaging one of the poppets, but no harm was caused to the hull. Subsequently, the ship would be towed to a fitting-out dock for completion. *National Archives*

Among the construction tasks performed during the fitting out of the *New Jersey* was the mounting of the 16-inch gun turrets. Here, turret 1, consisting of the gunhouse, the gun pit, and the machinery flat, is being lowered onto its barbette on January 13, 1943. The basic shell of the turret as it then existed was referred to as a weldment. The sides of the gunhouse as seen here were formed from 0.75-inch-thick special-treatment steel (STS); the front had 2.5-inch STS. Once the turret weldment was mounted on the barbette, the main armor would be bolted atop the STS plates: 9.5-inch Class A armor on the sides and 17-inch Class B armor on the front. Bolt holes have already been bored through the STS on the side of the gunhouse. The roof would receive 7.25-inch Class B armor; the rear of the gunhouse, 12-inch Class A. *National Archives*

Following five and a half months of fitting out, the battleship *New Jersey* was commissioned at the Philadelphia Naval Yard on May 23, 1943. At this time, the ship formally entered the service of the US Navy and now had the prefix "USS" (United States Ship) before its name. In this photo, Capt. Carl F. Holden, the first commanding officer of USS *New Jersey*, delivers remarks to the commissioning crew and spectators during the commissioning ceremony. The tall officer to his rear is RAdm. Milo Draemel, commandant of the Fourth Naval District, standing next to Governor and Mrs. Charles Edison. To the right is Cdr. Pete McDowell, first executive officer of the ship. *National Archives*

Officers of the crew of USS *New Jersey* hear the remarks of Capt. Carl Holden, standing to the rear of turret 3, during the commissioning ceremony. Forward of the turret are, from bottom to top, the aft Mk. 37 secondary-battery director, the aft Mk. 38 main-battery director, and the mainmast, topped with an SG surface-search radar antenna. Farther forward, atop the foremast, is the SK air-search radar antenna. *National Archives*

The bow of the *New Jersey* is viewed from the front on commissioning day, May 23, 1943. Flying from the staff on the forecastle is the jack of the United States of America, also called the union jack, with forty-eight stars on a field of blue. The black band below the Navy Blue paint on the hull is the boot topping, meant to disguise the oil and sludge that tended to cling to the waterline of the ship while in harbors. When the ship was fully loaded, the waterline would be along the boot topping. *National Archives*

A massive hammerhead crane towers above USS *New Jersey* on the day of its commissioning ceremony at the Philadelphia Naval Yard in May 1943. When the ship was launched, it was painted above the waterline in Light Gray. Now, it had been repainted in the Measure 21 scheme: Navy Blue (5-N) on all vertical surfaces, and Deck Blue (20-B) on horizontal surfaces. The ship's number, 62, is painted in white on the bow. *National Archives*

Sailors in dress whites and a number of civilians are gathered on the main deck and the upper levels on commissioning day. Interestingly, the hull below the black boot topping is of a bronze or gold color, not the usual red color. This is borne out in this photo and the preceding ones by comparing that bronze color with various red objects, such as the red stripes in the ensign and a red coat on a woman on the forecastle in this photo, suggesting that the apparent bronze coloration is not a distortion caused by seventy-five-year-old color film. *National Archives*

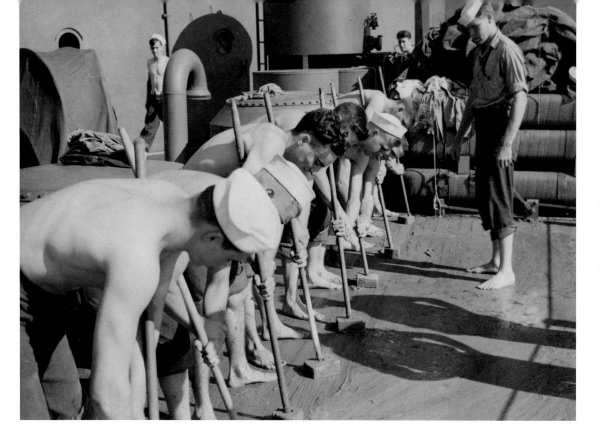

Sailors are holystoning a teak deck on USS *New Jersey* in July 1943. This was done in a regimented fashion, one plank at a time, by using a stick pressed into an indentation in the stone and rubbing it back and forth, to make a dull, weatherbeaten deck bright again. Often, sand and water were applied to the deck for extra abrasion. The holystones were sometimes made of sandstone, but those in common use in the US Navy at the time were of the same types of bricks used to line boilers. Later, the practice of holystoning was discontinued because it led to premature erosion of teak decks. *National Archives*

On July 8, 1943, in a view from the bridge of USS *New Jersey*, tugboats are maneuvering USS *New Jersey* away from its fitting-out dock at the Philadelphia Naval Yard. The battleship was about to embark on its first foray under its own power. The largest crane to the far right is the famous League Island Crane. Cloth covers are fitted over the muzzles of the 16-inch/50-caliber guns of turrets 1 and 2. *National Archives*

In a reverse companion image to the preceding photograph, the *New Jersey* is viewed from the forecastle while the ship is departing from the Philadelphia Naval Yard on July 8, 1943. In the foreground are the two gypsy heads: the windlasses for raising and lowering the anchors. Directly behind them are two single 20 mm antiaircraft guns, mounted on pedestals within round splinter shields. Sailors are crowded into a gun tub for a quad 40 mm antiaircraft gun mount on the roof of turret 2. To the immediate upper rear of that gun mount is the open navigating bridge, above which is the upper part of the conning tower and the forward fire-control tower, topped by the forward Mk. 38 director. *National Archives*

This third and final photo in a series documenting the departure of the *New Jersey* from the Philadelphia Naval Shipyard on July 8, 1943, was taken from the roof of turret 3 and shows the fantail, the two catapults, and the aircraft crane on the fantail. Two of the ship's Vought OS2U Kingfisher scout planes are on the catapults, and a third Kingfisher is on a dolly on the deck. These aircraft, which were assigned to VO-7, Battleship Division 7's scouting squadron, were used for scouting, spotting, and helping to correct the effect of the ship's gunfire, and general-purpose utility work. *National Archives*

A Vought OS2U Kingfisher scout plane has just been launched from USS *New Jersey* on July 20, 1943. The number "4" is on the fuselage. In the foreground are the aft smokestack and the mainmast. A 36-inch searchlight is under a cover on the platform on the smokestack. At the time, the ship was conducting its first shakedown cruise, in Delaware Bay. *National Archives*

The aft smokestack, the mainmast, and part of the rear of the main deck of USS *New Jersey* are viewed from the forward fire-control tower in July 1943, during the early part of the ship's shakedown period. At the top of the main mast is the rear SG surface-search radar antenna. On the smokestack, the 36-inch searchlights are in view with their covers removed.
National Archives

The guns of the USS *New Jersey* were fired for the first time during the shakedown cruise in Delaware Bay. In this July 21, 1943, photo, looking down on the port side of the ship from the upper part of the forward fire-control tower, the decks have been cleared of personnel prior to the firing of the guns, except for two sailors next to the flag bag in the lower center of the image. In the right foreground is a 40 mm antiaircraft gun mount. Lower down are two 5-inch/38-caliber gun mounts and two single 20 mm antiaircraft guns.
National Archives

USS *New Jersey* was conducting a shakedown cruise in Chesapeake Bay when it was photographed from an aircraft on August 5, 1943. At this time, the ship lacked the two 20 mm antiaircraft guns and their tub on the forecastle; these would be installed several months later. *National Archives*

This undated photograph almost certainly was taken an instant after the preceding one, since the sailors dressed in whites are grouped on the main deck identically, or nearly so, to the groups seen in the preceding shot. The 20 mm gun galleries abeam the rear of the superstructure would be replaced by two quadruple 40 mm antiaircraft gun mounts in September 1943. *National Archives*

During the return leg of a shakedown cruise to Trinidad in the Caribbean in August 1943, the fantail of USS *New Jersey* is viewed from the roof of turret 3. In the foreground, inside a splinter shield, is the Mk. 51 director and crew attached to the quadruple 40 mm antiaircraft gun mount on that turret roof. The Mk. 51 director consisted of a Mk. 14 gyro gunsight on a pedestal. The operator of the director tracked enemy aircraft and could remotely control one or more gun mounts. The mounts also could be controlled by their own crews under what was called local control. In the background are three OS2Us with covers over their engines and canopies. *National Archives*

USS *New Jersey* was photographed from an aircraft on September 6, 1943, while operating in Hampton Roads, Virginia. On that date, the crew of the *New Jersey* engaged in a battle problem while RAdm. Donald B. Beary, commander of Operational Training Command Atlantic, completed a two-day annual inspection of the ship. *National Archives*

This is the first in a series of five photos of the *New Jersey* at anchor in Hampton Roads, Virginia, on September 7, 1943. Here, a multitude of sailors in dress whites are gathered on the main deck. A boat on davits is casting an oversized shadow on the hull amidships. *National Archives*

Crewmen in a mix of dress whites, dress blues, and khakis are visible on deck in an aerial view from above the bow of the *New Jersey*. A canvas windscreen is rigged on the railing on the front of the forecastle. *National Archives*

USS *New Jersey* is seen from astern at Hampton Roads on September 7, 1943. Two of the ship's Vought OS2U Kingfishers are mounted on the starboard catapult; one Kingfisher is on the port catapult. Boat booms are deployed on each side of the fantail, for mooring the ship's boats while at anchor. *National Archives*

The *New Jersey* is viewed from above and off its port bow. On this date, the battleship would return to the Philadelphia Naval Yard, thus concluding its shakedown period. *National Archives*

In a final view of the *New Jersey* at Hampton Roads, Virginia, on September 7, 1943, in the background is the *Richelieu*, a French battleship that recently had been refitted at the Brooklyn Navy Yard and was conducting sea trials at the time of the photograph. Faintly visible on the shoreline beyond the *Richelieu* are the distinctive outlines of the historic Chamberlin Hotel, at Old Point Comfort, Virginia. *National Archives*

The newly enclosed navigating bridge is viewed from a close perspective from the port side of the main deck at Philadelphia in October 1943. The front of the enclosed bridge was curved, and the enclosure simply matched the original plan of the navigating bridge, with no expansion. The windows in the bridge could be opened by using hand cranks that raised or lowered the panes. *National Archives*

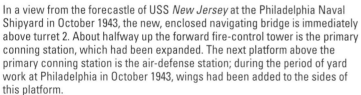

In a view from the forecastle of USS *New Jersey* at the Philadelphia Naval Shipyard in October 1943, the new, enclosed navigating bridge is immediately above turret 2. About halfway up the forward fire-control tower is the primary conning station, which had been expanded. The next platform above the primary conning station is the air-defense station; during the period of yard work at Philadelphia in October 1943, wings had been added to the sides of this platform.

Two of the Mk. 49 directors with Mk. 19 radars installed on the *New Jersey* in October 1943 were on platforms on the front corners of the aft fire-control tower. The starboard one is shown in this photograph taken October 29, 1943. At the lower left is an antenna trunk, and at the lower center is a 5-inch loading machine: a piece of equipment that allowed crewmen of the 5-inch/38-caliber gun mounts to practice loading the guns.

During the October 1943 refit, six Mk. 49 directors with Mk. 19 radar were mounted on the *New Jersey*, for controlling the antiaircraft batteries. An operator sat inside the rotating enclosure; an armored flap to the front of the operator's station is open. Visible inside are a telescopic sight and a radarscope. A hatch with a clear panel is on the rear of the compartment. On the right outside of the enclosure is the Mk. 19 antenna and transmitter/receiver. This Mk. 49 director was located in a splinter shield on the 05 level: the top of the conning tower is in the background.

Having undergone modernizations to the navigating bridge and the forward fire-control tower, and having taken on a load of ammunition (almost 100,000 pounds of antiaircraft ammo alone), *New Jersey* departed from the Philadelphia Naval Shipyard on October 13, 1943, and is seen in an aerial photo on that date. A close examination of the photo reveals that life rafts are stored on the sides of all three turrets and underneath the two catapults. *National Archives*

This image of USS *New Jersey* has been reported to have been taken in Boston in October 1943, but that information has not been independently confirmed. The *New Jersey* also returned to Boston for twelve days in December 1943, so it is conceivable the photo dates to that visit. The ship does exhibit the enclosed navigation bridge with the rounded front corners and the changes to the forward fire-control tower that were implemented earlier in October. *National Archives*

In late October 1943, USS *New Jersey* was dispatched on its first operational mission: to stand by in Casco Harbor, Maine, in the event its services were needed to combat the German battleships *Tirpitz* and *Scharnhorst*, then based in Norway. Here, the *New Jersey* kicks up spray as it plows through rough seas off the coast of Maine en route to Casco Harbor on October 23, 1943. *National Archives*

The *New Jersey* and its crew
spent a cold, uncomfortable
several months off Portland,
Maine, in the autumn of 1943. This
photo of the ship at anchor in the
chilly waters of Casco Bay is dated
November 25, 1943: Thanksgiving
Day. While standing on alert for a
possible sortie across the North
Atlantic against the German
battleships, the crew of the *New
Jersey* kept busy with an intensive
training regimen.
National Archives

The 16-inch/50-caliber guns of
turrets 1 and 2 are firing a
broadside during a training
exercise in Casco Bay, Maine, on
November 20, 1943. The two 20 mm
gun mounts and the two quadruple
40 mm gun mounts on the main
deck forward of turret 1 were part
of the ship as originally
constructed. *National Archives*

USS *New Jersey* is viewed from off its port bow while anchored in Casco Bay, Maine, on November 28, 1943. While anchored there, the ship's crew was able to go on leave in Portland.

The *New Jersey* is observed from closer to its port bow in Casco Bay on November 28, 1943. The small, taut chain running from the upper bow into the water was associated with the paravane system: paravanes are small, towed, submersible devices designed to cut the cables of submerged mines. *National Archives*

A Vought OS2U Kingfisher has just been launched from the port catapult of USS *New Jersey* off the coast of Maine on November 20, 1943. In the foreground are the aft smokestack and the mainmast, at the top of which is a small platform supporting an SG surface-search radar antenna. The ship finally received orders to sail south from Maine to Boston in mid-December after the German battleships failed to sortie from their harbors. *National Archives*

Transferred to the Pacific Fleet, USS *New Jersey* departed from the East Coast on January 2, 1944, and, after transiting the Panama Canal, arrived in the Ellice Islands in the Central Pacific on January 22. This photo of the *New Jersey* was taken on January 24 from an aircraft from the carrier USS *Bunker Hill* (CV-17) while the ship was en route to support the Marshall Islands Campaign. *National Archives*

A sailor wearing a helmet aboard USS *Iowa* (BB-61) watches as the 16-inch guns of its sister ship, USS *New Jersey*, unleash a barrage against Japanese positions on Tinian, in the Mariana Islands, on June 14 or 15, 1944. The two battleships were participating in the pre-invasion bombardment of that island. *National Archives*

USS *New Jersey* is departing from Pearl Harbor on August 24, 1944, after spending several weeks in port. The principal purpose of the visit was the modification of the ship's flag plot to the requirements of Adm. William F. Halsey, who would be making the *New Jersey* his flagship as commander of the Third Fleet. The work carried out at Pearl Harbor included replacement of all electrical wiring in the flag plot, installation of new communications gear, and other modernizations. (Note that this series of photos of the *New Jersey* making its sortie from Pearl Harbor was incorrectly dated August 31, 1944, on the photographs, and that error has been repeated in some published works.)

In a photograph taken over the starboard wing of an airplane, *New Jersey* has cleared the channel from Pearl Harbor and is proceeding into open water off Oahu on August 24, 1944. Sometime between January and June 1944, the forward SG surface-search radar antenna had been moved from the upper front of the forward fire-control tower to the top of a new mast to the rear of the SK "bedspring" air-search radar antenna atop the foremast; this new mast and SG antenna are seen clearly in this photo.

The *New Jersey* is viewed from above and astern as it goes out to sea following its August 1944 refit at Pearl Harbor, on August 24, 1944. A Vought OS2U Kingfisher scout plane is poised on each catapult, and a boat is stored on the deck to the rear of the 20 mm antiaircraft battery just aft of turret 3.

USS *New Jersey* is seen from another angle in an aerial view outside Pearl Harbor on August 24, 1944.

A patrol boat is approaching off the port bow of the *New Jersey* as it departs from Pearl Harbor on August 24, 1944. An admiral's barge is chugging alongside the starboard beam, below the quarterdeck.

This final view of USS *New Jersey* departing from Pearl Harbor on August 24, 1944, was taken from an aircraft relatively low off the port beam. One of the two Vought OS2U Kingfishers on the catapults would be lost during a landing accident four days later; the crewmen would be rescued. The ship's eventual destination on this voyage was the Philippines.

A Japanese prisoner of war is being marched along the deck of the *New Jersey*. He may have been a member of a group transferred to the battleship from the destroyer USS *Marshall* on September 12, 1944.
National Archives

Spray engulfs the forward part of USS *New Jersey* as it navigates a rough sea off the Philippines on November 8, 1944. The *Essex*-class aircraft carrier USS *Hancock* (CV-19) is visible in the background. The stern of the battleship is barely visible amid the huge waves. *National Archives*

In a companion image to the preceding photograph, taken on the same occasion, the forward hull of the *New Jersey* appears to have become submerged as the ship negotiates very rough water. *National Archives*

The USS *New Jersey* is the big ship slightly to the left of the center of this aerial photograph of ships of the Third Fleet at anchor in Ulithi Atoll, Caroline Islands, on November 6, 1944. The *New Jersey*'s sister ship, USS *Iowa*, is two ships to the rear, near the far right of the photo. Five *Essex*-class fleet carriers are anchored at the upper center of the photo. *National Archives*

On November 25, 1944, the *New Jersey* and other ships of Task Group 38.3 were attacked by *kamikazes* off the northern coast of Luzon in the Philippines. At the center of this shot, a Japanese *kamikaze* plane explodes as it crashes into the water ahead of the *New Jersey*, to the right side of the photo. *National Archives*

Nothing cheers up military personnel like mail call, and such is the case with these sailors of the *New Jersey* as they haul bags of mail just received, in December 1944. *National Archives*

Members of the *New Jersey*'s crew are pulling lines to haul in a whale boat in a November 1944 photograph. Next to them on a catapult is one of the ship's Vought OS2U Kingfishers, numbered "4" on the fuselage below the open canopy of the radioman/observer's cabin. *National Archives*

The aircraft crane on the fantail of the *New Jersey* is hoisting a Vought OS2U aboard following a mission in November 1944. The radioman/observer is standing gingerly on the wing, holding on to a line from the ship. *National Archives*

Members of the crew of USS *New Jersey* are attending a religious service on the fantail between the catapults on Thanksgiving Day 1944. To the far left is a portable altar. Riding at anchor in the background is USS *Iowa* (BB-61). *National Archives*

Adm. William F. Halsey Jr., commander, Third Fleet (third from left) enjoys Thanksgiving dinner on his flagship, USS *New Jersey*, while anchored at Ulithi Atoll on November 30, 1944. When the ship entered the atoll three days earlier, it had logged 36,185 miles since Admiral Halsey moved his flag to the *New Jersey* at Pearl Harbor three months earlier. *National Archives*

USS *New Jersey* is anchored at Ulithi Atoll in the Caroline Islands on December 8, 1944. A fleet anchorage and staging base for the campaign to liberate the Philippines, it also functioned as a rest-and-recreation area for US Navy personnel, where they could relax on a beach, play sports, drink a few beers, and enjoy being on terra firma. *National Archives*

A photographer aboard USS *New Jersey* snapped this shot of the *Allen M. Sumner*-class destroyer USS *Maddox* (DD-731) almost submerged in a huge swell during Typhoon Cobra on December 17 or 18, 1944. *National Archives*

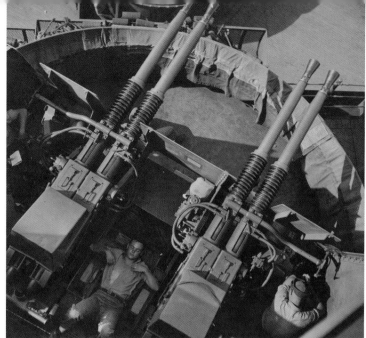

A member of the crew of a 40 mm antiaircraft gun mount on the *New Jersey* is taking advantage of a lull in the action to take a nap on the platform between the paired guns. Sailors' accounts of life on US Navy warships in World War II often strike a common chord: sleep often came at a steep premium. Between the heat of the sleeping quarters below decks and the frequent need to remain on alert at all hours of the day and night, it was very difficult to get sufficient sleep. Note the canvas covers over the 40 mm ammunition racks on the inside of the splinter shield. *National Archives*

Three members of the crew of USS *New Jersey* are cleaning and greasing 40 mm rounds while en route to the Philippines in December 1944. To the left are the cartridge deflectors on the rears of quadruple 40 mm antiaircraft guns; in the background are holders for four-round clips of 40 mm ammunition on the inside of the splinter shield for the gun mount. *National Archives*

Adm. William F. Halsey, second from left, is playing a game of deck tennis with members of his Third Fleet staff on the *New Jersey* in December 1944. The game is a mixture of tennis and quoits and is played with a ring, which is seen here in the air above the net to the front of Halsey. To the left is the side of the gunhouse of turret 1, with the hood for the right objective of the rangefinder jutting from it. *National Archives*

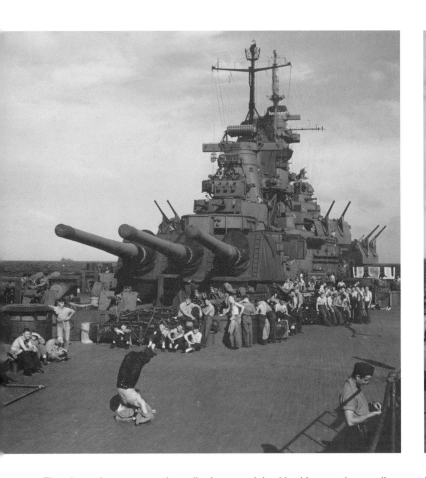

There's one in every crowd: a sailor is entertaining his shipmates by standing on his head on the main deck of the *New Jersey* aft of turret 3 during a break in the action in December 1944. Between the acrobatic crewman and the turret is the aft 20 mm gun gallery; the four shirtless sailors sitting on the deck to the rear of the splinter shield of that gallery are leaning against a bin holding floater nets. Distributed at several points around the ship, the floater nets were designed to float free of the battleship should it be sunk, giving surviving crewmen something to hang on to and keep them afloat until rescued. *National Archives*

In a December 1944 photograph at precisely the same spot and most likely on the same occasion as the preceding photograph, members of the crew of USS *New Jersey* are lined up on deck for mess. They are headed for a hatch in the deck toward the right, down to the crew's mess, which was one level below, on the second deck. *National Archives*

When you are tired enough, even a teak deck on a battleship has its comforts. Two enlisted men are taking a nap on the deck of the *New Jersey* during December 1944. Secured to racks on the side of the superstructure are tanks for oxyacetylene welding and brooms. *National Archives*

Five sailors are sitting on steel cables stored on the top of the barbette of a 16-inch/50-caliber gun turret on USS *New Jersey* during December 1944. Their heads are hidden by the overhang at the rear of the gunhouse of the turret. To the far left is a life raft, stored on the side of the gunhouse. *National Archives*

Members of the crew of the *New Jersey* are standing by at their battle stations on a fair-weather day in December 1944. To the left is the aft Mk. 37 secondary-battery director, while to the right is the aft fire-control tower, with a lookout standing by at a telescope on a small platform on the rear face of the tower. Note the ladder leading up to the platform. *National Archives*

Several crewmen are napping or relaxing on the main deck next to turret 3 during some off-duty time on the *New Jersey* in December 1944. To the upper left is the rear of the splinter shield of the 40 mm gun mount on the turret roof, and on the rear of the gunhouse is a bin for a floater net. In the background is one of the ship's Vought Kingfisher scout planes on the port catapult. *National Archives*

In a photo taken sometime before February 20, 1945, two crewmen are seen atop the gunhouse of one of the turrets of USS *New Jersey*. The photo provides a good view of the bloomers, or blast bags, which sealed off the gaps between the tubes of the 16-inch/50-caliber guns and the front of the gunhouse. The fronts of the bloomers were secured to the barrels with rings, and the rears of the bloomers were attached to the thick armor at the front of the gunhouse with metal frames called bucklers. *National Archives*

After a projectile has been rammed into this 16-inch/50-caliber gun on the *New Jersey*, crewmen are arranging bags of propellant on a tray for ramming into the chamber in November 1944. Six bags of propellant constituted a complete powder charge. The bags were fabricated from silk and contained smokeless powder. *National Archives*

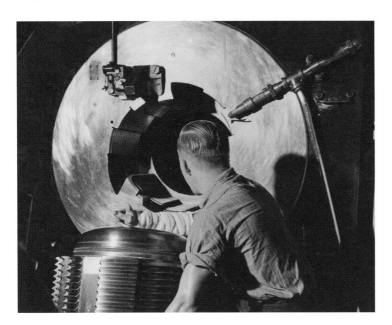

A gunner looks into the open chamber of a 16-inch/50-caliber gun aboard USS *New Jersey* preparatory to loading a round in November 1944. The breech plug is open, showing its interrupted-screw design. The dome-shaped structure on the breech plug is called the "mushroom." *National Archives*

In a final view in the series of late 1944 photos of the *New Jersey*'s crew at work and relaxing, two sailors are parbuckling a 16-inch shell, sliding it across the flat toward a shell hoist. The shells, lying upright with their flat bases resting on the bare-metal flat, were moved by the skilled use of a line and a capstan; the man to the right is managing the capstan and line while the man to the left steadies the shell. *National Archives*

A very weathered camouflage paint is apparent on the *New Jersey* while anchored at Ulithi Atoll on February 8, 1945. This is most apparent on the hull and was the result of the ship's spending many months at sea without having its paint refreshed. The contours of the bow's overhang is casting a large shadow over the side of the bow in the midday sun. *National Archives*

USS *New Jersey* is seen from amidships to the stern from USS *Borie* during a refueling at sea on March 16, 1945. A boom has been erected on the main deck of the *New Jersey* to support the fuel line. Note the dark-colored canvas cover over the Mk. 8 radar antenna mounted atop the Mk. 38 primary-battery director, to the upper left. *National Archives*

Sometimes, capital ships were called on to refuel smaller ships at sea. Such was the case in this series of photos of USS *New Jersey* refueling the destroyer USS *Borie* (DD-704) as Task Group 58.3 was underway from Ulithi to conduct air strikes against Kyushu, Japan, on March 16, 1945. In this view, the *New Jersey* is seen from the *Borie* from amidships forward, showing the two fuel lines rigged from the battleship to the destroyer. *National Archives*

The March 16, 1945, refueling operation is seen from the foredeck of USS *Borie*. Note the very baggy design of the blast bags, or bloomers, of the 5-inch/38-caliber gun mounts; these are the flexible covers that seal off the gap between the gun shield and the gun barrels, and they had to flex with the full elevation and depression of the guns. *National Archives*

On May 6, 1945, USS *New Jersey* arrived at Navy Yard Puget Sound, in Bremerton, Washington, for a long-overdue refitting and modernization. During its almost two-month sojourn there, its crew was able to go on leave in two shifts. The ship is seen here from above the forecastle on June 24, 1945. On that date, the ship was undergoing an inclining experiment to determine its new center of gravity following the modernization. *National Archives*

The *New Jersey* is seen from a different perspective during the inclining experiment on June 24, 1945, near the end of its modernization work at Navy Yard Puget Sound. In the foreground are the anchor chains, wound around the two gypsy heads, with the control wheels for the windlasses to the rear of the gypsy heads. Between the control wheels and the front of turret 1 are two 20 mm antiaircraft guns inside splinter shields, and two quad 40 mm antiaircraft guns inside splinter shields. A director for each 40 mm gun mount is elevated on the rear of the splinter shield.

One of the more visible changes made in the May–June 1945 modernization was the replacement of the enclosed navigating bridge with the rounded front with a new, larger one with a straight front. On the roof of turret 2, the Mk. 51 director to the front of the quadruple 40 mm gun mount received a new splinter shield, with a pointed rather than flat front, the result of a change from a square to a hexagonal plan for the splinter shield. During this yard time, the ship was repainted, in Measure 22 camouflage. This consisted of Navy Blue (5-NB) on the hull up to a horizontal line based on the lowest point of the main deck, #27 Haze Gray (5-H) on all remaining vertical surfaces and the masts, and Deck Blue (20-B) on all horizontal surfaces.
National Archives

A closer view is available of the new enclosure for the navigating bridge. Just below the open bridge of the primary conning station midway up the front of the forward fire-control tower is a tub containing a Mk. 57 director. There is another Mk. 57 director in a tub on the starboard side of this one, partially hidden by the forward Mk. 37 director. Both these directors are also visible in the preceding photo. These were radar-equipped, manually operated directors for controlling the 40 mm antiaircraft guns in blind-firing situations. Six Mk. 57 directors were installed on *New Jersey* in the May–June 1945 modernization, and they replaced the Mk. 49 directors installed in 1943. The large Mk. 3 fire-control radar antenna that had been atop the conning tower since the ship was commissioned had been deleted, and now a much-smaller Mk. 27 fire-control radar antenna was atop the rear part of the conning tower roof. The Mk. 12 radar antennas on top of the four Mk. 37 secondary-battery directors now were supplemented by Mk. 22 "orange-peel" parabolic height-finder antenna. *National Archives*

Continuing the look at the port side of the *New Jersey* during her June 24, 1945 inclining experiment, the battleship is seen from the forward smokestack to the fantail. Two new Mk. 57 directors, with dish radar antennas, are installed on platforms to the front of the aft smokestack. Clear views also are available of the twin 5-inch gun mounts, each of which has a detachable blast hood installed, for the protection of the mount captain.

The area between the smokestacks of USS *New Jersey* is depicted in a June 24, 1945, photo at Navy Yard Puget Sound. On the two round platforms on the front of the aft smokestack, just above the 40 mm gun mounts, are Mk. 57 directors. This photo also demonstrates the contrasting colors of the Measure 22 camouflage above the main-deck level. *National Archives*

An elevated view from the port side of the *New Jersey* on June 24, 1945, shows the ship from the rear of the aft smokestack to the stern. Two Mk. 57 directors have been mounted in tubs midway up the aft fire-control tower. On the main deck aft of the superstructure are temporary tracks, arranged laterally. These tracks supported weights that were moved from side to side during the inclining experiment. On the roof of turret 3 (this turret is trained to starboard) to the front of the 40 mm gun mount, a new, hexagonal splinter shield for the Mk. 51 director has been installed. This splinter shield is hinged at the bottom, and the six panels that compose the shield are folded down onto the turret roof. *National Archives*

A photograph of the *New Jersey* from above turret 3 facing forward on June 24, 1945, includes a clear view of the aft fire-control tower in the foreground. The Mk. 38 director still had the Mk. 8 fire-control radar antenna on top. A new, tripod-type mainmast had been installed on the aft smokestack during this modernization. *National Archives*

As seen from above the fantail of USS *New Jersey* on June 24, 1945, turret 3 is trained to starboard. At the bottom of the photo is part of the aft 20 mm antiaircraft-gun gallery and splinter shield, along with six 20 mm ammunition chests. Between the 20 mm gun gallery and turret 3 are two large ventilators and a hatch with a davit installed on its coaming, for lifting and lowering heavy objects in the hatch. Note the cube-shaped weights on trolleys on the tracks across the deck, used in the inclining experiments.
National Archives

In a final June 24, 1945 photo, the new Haze Gray paint on the catapults and the aircraft crane contrasts with the darker Deck Blue finish on the deck. Three sets of tracks for the inclining experiments that were being conducted on that date are on the deck aft of turret 3. Two quadruple 40 mm gun mounts and their associated Mk. 51 directors are situated on the fantail.
National Archives

The *New Jersey* is viewed from dead astern during a speed run on Puget Sound on June 30, 1945. During the May–June 1945 modernization, the old, rectangular SK air-search radar antenna was removed from the foremast, and the new, round, parabolic SK-1 antenna was mounted in its place. This feature is present in the photos of the *New Jersey* during the June 30, 1945, sea trials but is somewhat difficult to discern. *National Archives*

Much of the work performed on the *New Jersey* at Navy Yard Puget Sound in May and June 1945 consisted of repairs, maintenance, and improvements to its engineering plant. Once the modernization work was completed, the ship was subjected to sea trials on Puget Sound to ensure that all the mechanical systems were up to par. In this photo, USS *New Jersey* is making 18 knots during sea trials in Puget Sound on June 30, 1945. *National Archives*

As seen in a final view of USS *New Jersey* during sea trials on Puget Sound on June 30, 1945, the new, tripod mainmast on the aft smokestack had a new radar antenna on top of it: the SP height-finder radar, with an 8-foot-diameter dish. Above the top of the foremast, aft of the new SK-2 radar antenna, is an upper mast with an SG surface-search radar antenna on top. The aft SG radar antenna was on the mainmast, below the SP radar.

USS *New Jersey* is viewed from the port side while anchored off Blake Island in Puget Sound on July 2, 1945. On that date, the ship was taking on ammunition from barges, one of which is moored alongside her, abeam turret 2. Although not easily visible in this photo, a new type of scout plane had replaced the Vought OS2U Kingfishers: three Curtiss SC-1 Seahawks are onboard.

The two ammunition barges are moored to the sides of USS *New Jersey* in this view off the bow on July 2, 1945. On the hull, the demarcation is visible between the Navy Blue paint, which goes up to the level of the lowest point of the main deck, and the Haze Gray, which is on all vertical surfaces above the low point of the main deck. *National Archives*

In a view of the starboard side of the *New Jersey* off Blake Island on July 2, 1945, another barge is moored alongside it, adjacent to the forward turrets. Two SC-1 Seahawks were on the catapults, and a third one was on the fantail with its wings folded. *National Archives*

American sailors on a warship take in the impressive view of USS *New Jersey* at anchor at Yokosuka, Japan, after the end of World War II, in late December 1945. In the background, smoke billowing from the smokestack, is the Japanese battleship *Nagato*. *National Archives*

CHAPTER 3
Post–World War II and Korea

USS *New Jersey* departed from Yokosuka for the States on January 9, 1946. After a brief visit to San Francisco in early February and several months spent at Long Beach, California, the battleship was dispatched to the Puget Sound Naval Shipyard (as Navy Yard Puget Sound was renamed in 1946). This panoramic view of crewmen assembled on the port side of the *New Jersey* was taken at that shipyard while stationed there in April 1946. Several months earlier, the ship had been repainted in the typical USN postwar scheme of Haze Gray overall.
Naval History and Heritage Command

New Jersey returned to Puget Sound in June 1946, where it was tied up with a reduced crew of about 400. It then steamed to Bayonne, in its namesake state, being greeted on its May 23, 1947, arrival by Governor Alfred E. Driscoll and a host of other dignitaries. Starting in June, it took aboard midshipmen for training cruises in European waters and in July was operating in the Caribbean and Western Atlantic. At the end of the year, *New Jersey* put into Bayonne and began the process of inactivation, becoming part of the mothball fleet. On June 30, 1948, the process complete, *New Jersey* was decommissioned.

Its peaceful slumber was short lived, when, following the North Korean invasion of South Korea, *New Jersey* was reactivated. All the preservation measures carefully put in place in 1948 were removed, and on November 21, 1950, the ship was recommissioned. With many of its crew being recalled reservists, the battleship steamed to the Caribbean for training, then on April 16, 1951, stood out from Norfolk to Korea via Japan, arriving off the peninsula on May 17. VAdm. Harold Martin, commander of the 7th Fleet, broke his flag aboard *New Jersey*, and on May 20, it began shelling near Wonsan. It was during this action that its crew suffered their only casualty during the Korean War. A Korean shore battery found the mark, hitting *New Jersey*'s number 1 turret. One man was killed and two wounded by shell fragments. The mighty battleship responded with its 5-inch and 16-inch guns, obliterating the enemy positions.

From May 23 through 27, and again on May 30, *New Jersey* shelled Communist positions near Yangyang and Kansong. Among the targets were a bridge, ammunition dump, and railroad facilities, all of which were destroyed.

The Wonsan area was again targeted on June 4 and July 28, 1951. During the latter action, *New Jersey* was again fired upon by the enemy, which while achieving near misses did not connect. Once again, counterfire from *New Jersey* destroyed the North Korean positions.

During most of July and August, *New Jersey* continued its pounding of enemy positions, counting a dam, a bridge, multiple gun emplacements, railroad marshaling yards, and two ammunition dumps among the many targets destroyed by 5-inch and 16-inch gunfire.

In October, the mighty battleship fired at numerous targets along the Korean coast, with one spotter remarking that its men had done "every shot on target-most beautiful shooting I have seen in five years."

Wisconsin relieved *New Jersey* as flagship, and the "black dragon"—as it had been nicknamed during World War II, homage to its dark camouflage during that war—sailed for Norfolk and a much-needed overhaul.

Following the six-month-long overhaul, *New Jersey* took aboard midshipmen for a cruise, after which, on March 5, 1953, it left Norfolk again bound for the Pacific and service off Korea. On April 5, it relieved *Missouri* as flagship of the 7th Fleet. Less than a week later, it was again on the gun line, scoring seven direct hits on a North Korean communications center.

On May 23, 1953, *New Jersey* hosted the president of the Republic of Korea, Syngman Rhee, along with his wife, as well as Lt. Gen. Maxwell Taylor and various other dignitaries. Four days later, when again operating off Wonsan, the battleship was again taken under fire by shore installations. The only effect of the enemy action was to cause the battlewagon to respond both with its 5-inch and 16-inch batteries, annihilating the enemy positions. The next several weeks were spent in direct support of Allied troops operating on the coast. However, on July 11–12, the mighty battleship loosed one of the most ferocious bombardments of its career. On Saturday, July 11, its guns fire for nine hours and on the next day added seven more hours of shelling of enemy positions.

On July 26, *New Jersey* again fired on enemy positions near Wonsan, in what would be its final engagement of the war. President Rhee returned to the battleship on September 16 to present the Presidential Unit Citation to the 7th Fleet.

On October 14, *New Jersey* was relieved as flagship by *Missouri* and the next day stood out for Norfolk, arriving November 14.

Attached to the 6th Fleet, and operating out of Norfolk, *New Jersey* conducted training cruises and took part in NATO exercises until it steamed to New York Navy Yard for decommissioning on December 14, 1956. The battleship was mothballed and placed in reserve at Bayonne on August 21, 1957.

In the summer of 1947, USS *New Jersey* transported a contingent of US Naval Academy students on a midshipmen's cruise to Europe. In June and July the ship visited several ports in the United Kingdom, and this view apparently was taken at one of them. An interesting piece of cargo is stored on the main deck adjacent to the rear part of the superstructure: a carry-all vehicle.

Upon landing on the ocean on July 27, 1947, a Curtiss SC-1 Seahawk scout plane has taxied up to a sea sled towed by USS *New Jersey* and will soon be hoisted by crane up to the fantail, for remounting on a catapult. To the far right, sailors are standing by in the armored tub for the quad 40 mm gun mount on the starboard side of the fantail of the battleship; note the slots on the rack inside the tub for storing clips of 40 mm ammunition. *National Archives*

US Naval midshipmen and reservists relax on the foredeck of USS *New Jersey* while the ship is being refueled at sea by the tanker USS *Chemung* (AO-30) in northern European waters on July 16, 1947. Two fuel lines are rigged from the tanker to the battleship. *National Archives*

The battleship *New Jersey* is moored at the Military Ocean Terminal at Bayonne, New Jersey, on June 1, 1949, one year after being decommissioned and placed in the New York Group, Atlantic Reserve Fleet. Boats and several storage sheds are on the aft part of the main deck. This terminal also served as the Navy Yard Annex. *National Archives*

The *New Jersey* is viewed from dockside at the Military Ocean Terminal at Bayonne on September 18, 1950. With the Korean War now underway, the ship was about to be "de-mothballed," recommissioned, and returned to active service. *National Archives*

A sailor standing on the roof of turret 1 watches as a crane at the Military Ocean Terminal at Bayonne lifts a protective dome from the quadruple 40 mm antiaircraft gun mount on the roof of turret 2 on the *New Jersey* on September 26, 1950. The placard on the front of turret 2, which reads, "US [*sic*] NEW JERSEY," had been installed recently. *Naval History and Heritage Command*

Navy personnel are "de-mothballing" the 16-inch/50-caliber guns of turret 1 of the *New Jersey* at Bayonne in October 1950. Sailors are pulling large sheets of tape off the muzzles, revealing muzzle plugs underneath. Note the plug that covers the gap between the front of the gunhouse of the turret and the left 16-inch gun tube. *National Archives*

On November 21, 1950, USS *New Jersey* was recommissioned in a ceremony at Bayonne. Fleet Admiral William F. "Bull" Halsey returned on that date to his former flagship to deliver the main speech. Here, members of the mess crew are serving sailors on recommissioning day. *National Archives*

On November 3, 1950, the *New Jersey* is undergoing work to ready it for recommissioning. Turret 1 still had the prominent hoods for the rangefinder objectives on the sides of the gunhouse; these hoods would be removed soon during preparations for reactivating the ship, since the rangefinder was to be removed from that turret. *National Archives*

USS *New Jersey* cruises in open waters off the Korean coast on May 18, 1951, the day after the battleship arrived in the Korean waters and two days before its first bombardment mission. This view shows clearly the side of the gunhouse of turret 1, from which the rangefinder recently had been removed. *Naval History and Heritage Command*

On May 25, 1951, the *New Jersey* operates in the Sea of Japan. Four days earlier, on May 21, the ship came under fire from an enemy battery in a cave on the Kalmagak Peninsula in Wonsan Harbor, Korea. One shell detonated on turret 1, while shrapnel from another shell killed Seaman Robert Osterwind, who was the only member of the crew ever killed in action on the *New Jersey*. The *New Jersey*'s guns soon zeroed in on the enemy battery and destroyed it. Battle damage was not enough to keep the ship out of action. *National Archives*

The center and left 16-inch/50-caliber guns of turret 2 of USS *New Jersey* have just fired a salvo at Communist forces along the eastern coastline of the Korean peninsula on June 6, 1951. *National Archives*

Geisha girls on a bandstand wave to members of the crew of the *New Jersey* upon arrival at the US Navy base at Yokosuka, Japan, on May 16, 1951. Note the vision slots with armored flaps lowered on the conning tower above the open bridge of the primary conning station. *National Archives*

Navy ammunition handlers and Korean laborers are easing a 16-inch shell down to a dolly next to turret 2 on USS *New Jersey* somewhere on the coast of Korea on August 3, 1951. From here, the shell will be lowered down into a magazine deep inside the hull. Above the turret is the enclosed navigating bridge, over which are the Mk. 12 radar antenna with Mk. 22 "orange peel" antenna on the right side, atop the forward Mk. 37 secondary-battery director. To the rear of those antennas is the forward fire-control tower, with the primary conning station toward the bottom and the air-defense station and the Mk. 38 primary-battery director toward the top. *National Museum of Naval Aviation*

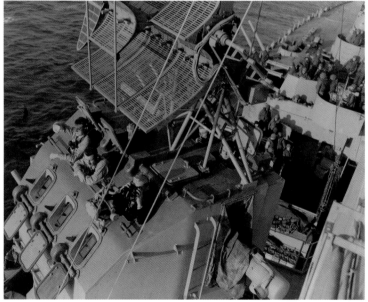

Five crewmen of one of the four Mk. 37 secondary-battery directors on USS *New Jersey* are scanning for Communist targets on the Korean coast on May 20, 1951. In the three front hatches, from left to right, are the trainer, the pointer, and the control officer. In the rear hatches are, left to right, the rangefinder operator and the assistant control officer. Jutting from the side of the director is the left objective of the rangefinder. Above the director are the Mk. 12 and Mk. 22 radar antennas. *National Archives*

In mid-May 1951, USS *New Jersey* is steaming toward the coast of Korea. From this angle, there is a clear view of the fantail without the catapults, which were removed after World War II. The aircraft crane remained in place. The ship was serving at that time with Task Force 77. *National Museum of Naval Aviation*

One of the 5-inch/38-caliber guns of USS *New Jersey* has just fired at an enemy target at Kosong on the Korean coast on September 13, 1951. The US Navy was keeping that area under constant bombardment. On the rear of the roof of the gun mount is a blast hood, to protect the gun captain when looking out of the hatch on the roof. *National Archives*

Smoke erupts on a hill along the Korean coast from shells from USS *New Jersey* during an October 1951 bombardment. Shellings by the *New Jersey* helped interdict Communist supply lines along the coast and disrupted and destroyed troop concentrations. *National Archives*

The 16-inch/50-caliber guns of USS *New Jersey* have just fired a broadside salvo against enemy forces near the 38th parallel in Korea on November 10, 1951. The targets are the smoke-covered areas on the hilltop to the left. Note the shock waves on the water on the port side of the battleship. *National Archives*

USS *New Jersey* steams in Korean waters on April 2, 1953. By this time, the small number "62" on the ship's bow had been replaced by a large number "62," in white, with black shadowing. *National Archives*

Sikorsky HO3S-1 USN, Bureau Number 124352, from Helicopter Utility Squadron 1 (HU-1) is lifting off of the helipad on the fantail of USS *New Jersey* on April 14, 1953. The introduction of helicopters into the fleet after World War II obviated the need for battleship-based scout planes. Helicopters not only provided a platform for scouting and artillery spotting but also lent themselves to ferrying personnel, delivering supplies, evacuating wounded, and other utility tasks. *National Archives*

In a view from the forecastle of USS *New Jersey*, the *Fletcher*-class destroyer USS *Trathen* (DD-530) is coming alongside to receive a load of mail from the battleship, in Korean waters on April 17, 1953. Sometime in the interval between spring 1951 and spring 1953, the forward Mk. 37 director, above the navigating bridge, had been equipped with a dish radar antenna, but the two Mk. 37 directors abeam the forward smokestack still had the old Mk. 12 and Mk. 22 radar antennas. Also worthy of notice is that the open bridge of the primary conning station, just above the aforementioned dish antenna, recently had been remodeled; the air deflector had been removed, and a glass windscreen with six tilted support struts had been installed. *National Archives*

Two sister ships of the *Iowa* class, USS *Missouri* (BB-63) on the left and USS *New Jersey* (BB-62), are moored side by side in Yokosuka Harbor, Japan, in April 1953. Although there are variations in the two ships (note the lack of side wings on the air-defense station of the *Missouri* near the top of the forward fire-control tower), both ships now were equipped with SPS-6 air-search radar and SG-6 surface-search radar on the foremasts. *National Archives*

Personnel in a radio room in USS *New Jersey* are receiving radio messages and typing them for distribution to the proper members of the staff during the spring of 1953. *National Archives*

Three members of the engineering division of USS *New Jersey* are at work in Engine Room No. 3 on April 21, 1953. To the left is Fireman John M. Hernandez, the throttleman, who controls engine rpm. To his side are two machinist's mate firemen, serving as talkers: James Cronin and Robert E. Plank. *National Archives*

A crewman of the *New Jersey* is collecting spent 5-inch casings following a fire mission against enemy targets on the Korean coast in the spring of 1953. In the background is a ship's boat with "NJ" marked on the bow. *National Archives*

Two members of the crew of the lower projectile flat deep below turret 2 of the *New Jersey*, Seaman Arthur G. Longley on the left and Gunner's Mate 1st Class Henry P. Castles, are parbuckling a shell on April 9, 1953. Parbuckling is a procedure for sliding upright 16-inch projectiles from their storage spots across the flat to projectile hoists, using a capstan and line. *National Archives*

On April 14, 1953, President Syngman Rhee of the Republic of Korea visited USS *New Jersey* at Pusan Harbor. In a photo taken just before President Rhee boarded the ship, US Ambassador Ellis O. Briggs, dressed in civilian clothes at the center of the photo, walks past the ship's band and honor guard while sailors in dress blues man the rails. A winch with two capstans is to the front of the band. On the roof of turret 3 to the right is a boom and sheave, for lowering ammunition below decks. *National Archives*

To the left, signalmen are operating a 24-inch searchlight on the signal bridge on the starboard side of the flag level of USS *New Jersey* on April 18, 1953. Next to this searchlight are a 12-inch searchlight and a binocular telescope. To the upper right is the side of the enclosed navigating bridge. *National Archives*

Crewmen of the *New Jersey* are in their racks in the spring of 1953. In the three-tier rack to the right, the top sailor is reading a NAVPERS training manual, the middle man is holding a ukulele, and the bottom man is reading a pulp western by William Colt MacDonald titled *Six-Gun Melody*. *National Archives*

Chief petty officers of USS *New Jersey* engage in a game of acey-deucey in a wardroom. *National Archives*

As the 1950s progressed, the twin threats of nuclear weapons and increasingly sophisticated airpower made the future of the battleship seem increasingly precarious. One by one, the old battlewagons were placed in "mothballs," on inactive status. In this image, tugboats are maneuvering alongside the battleship *New Jersey* at Norfolk, Virginia, on December 13, 1956, as it prepares to sail north to the Brooklyn Navy Yard in New York, where it will be inactivated. *Naval History and Heritage Command*

CHAPTER 4
Reactivation for Vietnam

In early 1962, the decision was made to close the reserve fleet facility at Bayonne. Plans were put in place to tow the *New Jersey*, as well as other vessels, to the Philadelphia Navy Yard, with the relocation operation beginning in May.

New Jersey languished in Philadelphia, its spaces sealed and the dehumidification equipment preserving the ship, while around the world US forces were engaged in heavy fighting in Vietnam. Initially, cruisers were used; however, the Navy had relatively few cruisers armed with guns in the fleet, the type having been forsaken in favor of guided-missile cruisers.

Faced with the expense—both in lives and monetarily—of heavy air support, various leaders both in and outside the military looked toward the Navy for help. Shore bombardment, now called Naval Gunfire Support, provided a means to deliver heavy artillery—sometimes continuous—where needed, reduced cost of operation, and resulting in fewer casualties. While some, including notably Senator Richard Russell of the Senate Armed Services and Appropriations Committees, favored the return of the battleship, others, including notably Adm. David MacDonald, Chief of Naval Operations, fiercely opposed this.

The cause of the battleship advocates was bolstered when the 8-inch gunned cruiser USS *Canberra* (CAG-2, previously CA-70), was hit by a shore battery March 2, 1967, injuring several sailors. The battleships had the range—and the heavy armor—to avoid similar issues. On May 11, 1967, the Navy sought permission to reactivate the *New Jersey*. At the end of the month, McNamara ordered a study to determine the cost and feasibility of reactivate the *New Jersey*, with only modest modernization from its Korean War condition. On August 1, the day after MacDonald's retirement, the decision to return *New Jersey* to service was announced.

The wisdom of this decision was reinforced a month later, when on September 1, 1967, the heavy cruiser USS *St Paul* (CA-73) was also hit by North Vietnamese shore batteries.

The survey of the vessel prior to the official decision to reactivate the ship had done much of the preparatory work, yet considerable work remained, including removal of the 20 mm and 40 mm gun batteries. For purposes both of speed and economy, the reactivation was directed to be "austere." This led some to wonder if all the guns were to be reactivated, and even if the entire engineering plant would be returned to service.

This matter was put to rest on January 18, 1968, when the ship's newly arrived prospective commanding officer, Capt. J. Edward Snyder Jr., met with his officers and announced: "Gentlemen, let there be no doubt in your minds. *New Jersey* will be a battleship and nothing less."

Although it was thirteenth on the work list at the Philadelphia Naval Shipyard, getting the battleship off the coast of Vietnam was a priority for Capt. Snyder, who was able to appeal to workers at the shipyard, where the battleship had been built decades before, to step up the pace.

On March 27, 1968, on the second day of its shakedown cruise, *New Jersey* was able to make 35.2 knots and maintain that speed for six hours, setting a battleship speed record. The run was interrupted only by the captain ordering "All back emergency" as a final test for the revived engineering plant.

Having passed the shipyard trials, on April 6, 1968, *New Jersey* was recommissioned. It left Philadelphia on May 16, bound for Long Beach by way of Norfolk. Leaving California on September 2, after brief stops at Pearl Harbor and Subic Bay, on September 30, it opened fire on targets in Vietnam for the first time. Being described as a "sailor's sailor" who was keenly interested in the welfare and morale of his crew, Capt. Snyder had two of the disused 40 mm gun tubs sealed shut and the interiors painted pale blue, providing *New Jersey*'s crew with two small swimming pools.

The veteran warship operated off the coast of Vietnam until April 1, 1969, providing much-needed—and appreciated—gunfire support for troops ashore. Capt. Snyder, whose leadership style elicited considerable loyalty and motivation from his crew, was also fond of bringing ground troops aboard. This provided the troops a respite from field conditions—specifically safety, security, hot showers and meals (with head-of-the-line privileges), and laundry services. Equally important, those troops, deeply appreciative of the support from the battleship, were effusive in their praise for the crew, motivating them to excel.

SSgt. Robert Gauthier summed up the Marines' feelings for *New Jersey* in an interview over the ship's TV system: "You are doing more to improve the morale of the men on the beach than anything else in the war. Every time we go on patrol, someone says, 'The Big One is out there. Nobody better mess with us or she'll get them.' You are saving lives out here . . . American lives. And we thank you."

Capt. Snyder was also remembered as having a sense of humor. While operating off Vietnam, *New Jersey* was challenged by a small US Navy ship, flashing the signal "Unknown vessel identify yourself." Since Capt. Snyder had ordered that no messages were to go out without his personal approval, the officer of the deck ignored the challenge, as well as the repeated challenge a few minutes later. When the ship issued the third challenge, it was more forceful, stating "unknown vessel—identify yourself or we will open fire." With that, Capt. Snyder was summoned. Annoyed

that the captain of another US Navy vessel could not distinguish the radar signature of the enormous battleship from that of a Vietcong gunboat, he ordered the *New Jersey*'s 24-inch searchlight to send back the terse message: "OPEN FIRE WHEN READY— FEAR GOD—DREADNOUGHT."

During its first deployment off Vietnam, *New Jersey* fired 5,688 rounds of 16-inch shells, and 14,891 rounds of 5-inch shells—12,000,000 pounds of ammunition. For perspective, this was only 1,500 main battery rounds less than it had fired in combat both in World War II and Korea combined. The ammunition usage likely would have been higher, if it were not for the McNamara-imposed limit of sixty-five 16-inch rounds per day.

On April 29, 1969, *New Jersey* steamed for Long Beach, California, for refit, and rest for the crew in preparation for a second deployment. With the refit complete and the stores replenished, in July it steamed to Pearl Harbor on a training cruise before returning to San Diego late in the month. Shortly thereafter, Capt. Robert Peniston reported aboard to prepare to relieve Capt. Snyder, who was to take the battleship back to Vietnam. The day after reporting aboard, Capt. Peniston was informed that rather than returning to Vietnam, the battleship would be returning to mothballs, a move that now is widely recognized as political rather than tactical.

At the change-of-command ceremony, a frustrated Capt. Snyder remarked, "War is hell, and it is also expensive, and the American people have tired of the expense of defending freedom."

A few weeks later, at the decommissioning ceremony on December 17, 1969, Capt. Peniston eloquently admonished: "Rest well, yet sleep lightly, and hear the call, if again sounded, to provide firepower for freedom."

The government began making moves in early 1967 to reactivate the battleship *New Jersey* for service in the Vietnam War, and in August of that year the Department of Defense made the project official. The forward end of the *New Jersey* is seen here in a nest of deactivated ships prior to reactivation, moored on the port side of the battleship *Wisconsin* (BB-64) at Philadelphia Naval Shipyard in June 1967. Note on the roof of turret 2 the folded-down splinter shield for the director for the 40 mm gun mount farther aft on the turret roof. *National Archives*

The fantail of the *New Jersey* is seen from the port side of turret 3 at Philadelphia in June 1967. The aircraft crane has been folded down onto the deck, and dome-shaped shelters are over the 40 mm gun mounts on the fantail. The T-shaped structure to the side of the turret is an enclosure for a winch. *National Archives*

Turret 3 and the aft part of the main deck are in view in this June 1967 photo of the *New Jersey*. The box-shaped shelter on the deck aft of the turret was used as a movie-projection booth for showing motion pictures on the fantail. The topmast of the foremast is stored on the turret roof. *National Archives*

On June 11, 1967, the process of taking the *New Jersey* out of mothballs has begun. The battleship *Wisconsin* has been towed out into the Delaware River, away from its place in the nest of ships abeam the *New Jersey*, and the tugboats are moving up to the *New Jersey* to pull it away from its position, to relocate it in order to commence its reactivation work. To the right is the *Essex*-class aircraft carrier *Antietam* (CV-36), part of the reserve fleet at this time. *National Archives*

Tugboats have pulled the *New Jersey* free of the nest of battleships in which it had been stored at the Philadelphia Naval Shipyard, on June 11, 1967. The bow of the *Wisconsin* is visible to the left, and the battleship *Iowa* remains moored to the dock. *National Archives*

Tugboats jockey to keep the *New Jersey* on course as it makes its way on the Delaware River to Pier 4 on June 11, 1967. In the background is the League Island hammerhead crane, which had towered over the *New Jersey* at the time of its fitting-out and commissioning in 1943. *National Archives*

A short time after the preceding photo was taken, tugboats are moving the *New Jersey* forward to Pier 4 (right background) at the Philadelphia Naval Shipyard, where work to prepare it for recommissioning will soon commence. *US Navy*

The *New Jersey* is now moored alongside Pier 4 at the Philadelphia Naval Shipyard on June 11, 1967, where work soon will begin on modernizing it for reactivation. The hull is riding high in the water, with all the boot topping around its waterline being above water. The ship will settle deeper in the water as it is being refitted and resupplied. *National Archives*

One of the protective domes placed over a 40 mm antiaircraft gun mount when the ship was placed in mothballs is observed from above.

Inside the massive door of the conning tower at the 04 level (that is, the fourth level above the main deck) is the ship's conning station, or pilothouse. The armor of the conning tower is 17.3 inches thick, fabricated from segments of Class B armor. Above the door is a placard identifying the compartment number. These placards allow personnel to determine their location at any point in the ship. This identifies the compartment as the ship and flag conning station. The number at the top of the placard, 04-87-1, means that it is on the 04 level, at frame 87, and the first compartment to the starboard of the ship's centerline.

The battleship *New Jersey* is being floated into a dry dock at the Philadelphia Naval Shipyard on September 20, 1967, during its refitting. Some scaffolding has been erected at various places around the superstructure for the use of workers during the modernization process. *National Archives*

A portable scaffold is set up next to turret 2 of the *New Jersey* during its time in dry dock in Philadelphia in September 1967. The structure to the front of the barbette of turret 2, with the elbow vent on the roof, was the First Division office. Near the top of the side of the gunhouse of turret 1, at the upper right, the armored plug is visible where the rangefinder hood had been removed in the early 1950s. *National Archives*

After the *New Jersey* was floated into dry dock, the gate was closed and the water pumped out, allowing the hull to settle on carefully positioned keel blocks under the centerline of the ship and on bilge blocks to the sides of the keel blocks. In this view from off the port stern, the keel blocks and the port bilge blocks are visible, as are the rudders and three of the propellers. *National Archives*

A worker at the Philadelphia Naval Shipyard poses next to the center tube of turret 1 during September 1967. With the blast bags removed, it is possible to get a sense of the thickness of the front of the gunhouse: 17 inches of armor over 2.5-inch special-treatment steel (STS).

The *New Jersey* is observed from astern at Pier 4 during modernization in September 1967. With the protective domes removed from the antiaircraft gun mounts, the quad 40 mm guns on the fantail are visible, although their barrels had been removed. *National Archives*

One of the *New Jersey*'s twin 5-inch/38-caliber gun mounts is viewed from above in September 1967. On the sides of the shield of the gun mount are sight hoods, for use when the mount is being operated under local control. Below the hood on each side is an access panel for mechanical equipment related to the gun mount. A blast hood is installed over the gun captain's hatch on the roof. Another twin 5-inch/38-caliber gun mount is to the right.

The battleship is viewed off its port bow in September 1967. Although the major exterior structures were intact, there were thousands of smaller fixtures, fittings, and rigging to install before the ship would be operationally ready.

The *New Jersey* is viewed from the foredeck as work progresses in dry dock at Philadelphia in September 1967. The quadruple 40 mm gun mount, minus its barrels, remains in place in the tublike starboard splinter shield to the rear of the gypsy heads, but the 40 mm gun mount is missing from the tub on the port side of the deck.

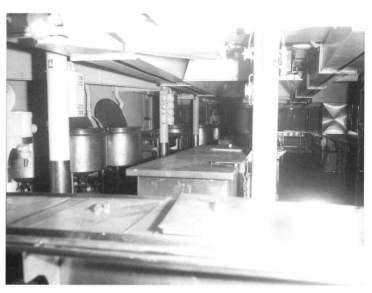

This is a galley in the *New Jersey* as it appeared in September 1967 during the modernization work. To the left are several cooking vats. *National Archives*

In a reverse view of the preceding photo, the foredeck is seen from the roof of turret 2. In the foreground on the roof is the mount for a gun director; the six panels of the splinter shield of the director are folded down. In the background, to the front of the guns of turret 1, are the two splinter shields for the 40 mm gun mounts along with the elevated tubs for the related directors.

Equipment is shown in an unidentified compartment in the *New Jersey* in September 1967. *National Archives*

A canvas cover is fitted over the muzzle of the left 16-inch/50-caliber gun of turret 1 in this September 1967 photograph. Running across the main deck to the front of the turret is the breakwater, which deflected waves when they engulfed the main deck.

The *New Jersey* is viewed from the forward fire-control tower during the final days of its period in Dry Dock No. 3 at the Philadelphia Naval Shipyard; the ship left the dry dock on January 13, 1968. At the bottom of the photo is the roof of the conning tower, to the immediate front of which is an open bridge. Below are turrets 1 and 2; the 40 mm guns have been removed from the roof of turret 2 and from the two tubs on the foredeck. Straddling the foredeck but not easy to see in this photo is a frame that will support the antenna array for the Naval Tactical Data System (NTDS), a new, computerized system for detecting and tracking multiple targets and selecting weapons.
National Archives

Floodlights illuminate the *New Jersey* while work continues in Dry Dock No. 3 at Philadelphia in mid-January 1968. Fresh paint is visible on the bow, and a new, box-shaped structure has been added to the upper part of the forward fire-control tower: an electronic countermeasures (ECM) control compartment, with a redesigned air-defense station on its roof. *US Navy*

The *New Jersey* cruises on the placid waters of Delaware Bay after completing its sea trials on March 26, 1968. In less than two weeks the ship would be recommissioned. The new NTDS antenna is in the foreground, situated on the frame straddling the forecastle. The ship sported a multitude of new antennas and sensors, installed during the 1967–68 modernization, including those for radar, communications, and electronic countermeasures. *US Navy*

With the Delaware Memorial Bridge in the background, the newly modernized and refitted battleship *New Jersey* sails under its own power down the Delaware River en route to sea trials prior to its reactivation on March 25, 1968. The new ECM control compartment is prominent toward the top of the forward fire-control tower. *US Navy*

On April 6, 1968, USS *New Jersey* is being recommissioned for the second time (the first time having been in November 1950). The scene is Philadelphia Naval Shipyard, with the League Island Crane towering over the proceedings. A freshly marked helipad is prominent on the fantail. The ceremonies were not without incidents: Vietnam War protesters picketed the recommissioning on land and in boats on the Delaware River. *Naval History and Heritage Command*

Twelve days after the recommissioning of USS *New Jersey*, the 16-inch/50-caliber guns are being test-fired in the Atlantic Ocean. To the lower right is the upper part of the forward Mk. 37 director, with its Mk. 25 dish radar antenna. To the front of the director is the roof of the conning tower, with several periscopes jutting through it.

Crewmen of USS *New Jersey* are cleaning the bore of the center 16-inch/50-caliber gun of turret 1 during a three-day gunnery practice session in the Atlantic off the Virginia Capes on May 24, 1968. This was part of the battleship's underway training before being deployed to combat. *National Archives*

USS *New Jersey* is receiving ammunition from barges alongside its port beam at Norfolk, Virginia, in May 1968. One barge is equipped with a substantial crane. Jutting from the sides of the new ECM compartment on the forward fire-control tower are frames to support antennas for the ULQ-6 ECM system, which detected approaching antiship missiles and jammed their radar-guidance equipment. The foretop now had an SPS-6C air-search radar, an SPS-10 surface-search radar, and radomes for ECM equipment. *US Navy*

The *New Jersey*, on the right, is in the Pedro Miguel Locks of the Panama Canal alongside a merchant ship on June 4, 1968. The locks are 110 feet wide, and the *New Jersey* has a beam of 108 feet, so there was a mere 2 feet to spare. *US Navy*

Sailors wearing whites crowd the rails and any available horizontal space as USS *New Jersey* negotiates the Miraflores Locks of the Panama Canal on June 4, 1968. The ship's number, 62, is painted in white with black shadowing on each side of the bow. *US Navy*

The full fury of a broadside salvo from all nine of USS *New Jersey*'s 16-inch/50-caliber guns is apparent in this aerial view taken off San Clemente Island, California, during a live-firing exercise on June 25, 1968. The white markings on the helipad are visible on the fantail, and the tubs for the 40 mm gun mounts and their directors are still present on the foredeck. *Naval History and Heritage Command*

Hardhat-wearing crewmen of USS *New Jersey* are guiding a pallet of six powder tanks for the ship's 16-inch/50-caliber guns down to the main deck during an underway replenishment (UNREP) from USS *Haleakala* (AE-25), the *Nitro*-class ammunition ship in the background, in the Gulf of Tonkin, off Vietnam, on October 4, 1968. The ammunition was transferred from the *Haleakala* to the *New Jersey* by means of a highline. The battleship had been engaged in shelling enemy targets along the coast since September 30. *National Archives*

A sailor leans against powder tanks, canisters containing powder charges for USS *New Jersey*'s 16-inch/50-caliber guns, during August 1968. During that month, the ship was at Long Beach Naval Shipyard, California, undergoing final measures to prepare it for combat in the Vietnam War. *National Archives*

This undated view of USS *New Jersey* steaming on the high seas during the Vietnam is thought to have been taken in 1968. Worthy of notice are the large awning over the main deck on the starboard side of turret 2 and the small awning over the open bridge of the primary conning station, midway up the forward fire-control tower. The two 40 mm gun tubs on the foredeck had been removed in California in the summer of 1968. There are several aerial color photos of the ship off Oahu in early September 1968 that show the same configuration of awnings, and those photos have a similar "feel" to this one, so it is possible this photo dates to early September 1968. *US Navy*

The right gun of turret 3 of USS *New Jersey* has just fired a 1,900-pound shell against an enemy position in January 1969. The target was approximately 20 miles away. An antenna is jutting from the side of the mainmast, adjacent to the top of the aft smokestack. *US Navy*

A 30-foot crater created by a 16-inch shell from the *New Jersey* is viewed from directly above. The blast also cleared vegetation within a 150-yard radius.

The following sequence of three photos documents the effects of a shelling by the 16-inch/50-caliber guns of USS *New Jersey* in January 1969. Here, a shell has just detonated on a coastal plain already pocked by a multitude of shell craters.

At the center of this aerial photo is an enemy bunker, which soon will be destroyed by shells from USS *New Jersey*.

During March 1969, the 16-inch/50-caliber guns of USS *New Jersey* are firing at Vietcong positions along the coastline of South Vietnam. During its 1968–69 deployment to Vietnam, the *New Jersey* fired over 5,000 16-inch shells and approximately 15,000 5-inch rounds, knocking out thousands of enemy strongpoints. Its big guns had a reach of up to 23 miles inland. *US Navy*

Following its deployment to Vietnam, USS *New Jersey* visited Subic Bay, Philippines, and Yokosuka, Japan, before sailing for Long Beach, California. When the ship was nearing Long Beach, its orders were changed, and it was sent back to the Far East in response to a brewing crisis in Korea. In this photo, tugboats are assisting *New Jersey* into Yokosuka Naval Base, Japan, on April 22, 1969. The ship was reprovisioned there before sailing to an assigned area at sea to await developments in the crisis. When the crisis failed to turn into open hostilities, the *New Jersey* sailed for Long Beach, where it arrived on March 5, 1969.

Although the *New York Times* and other media outlets reported in May 1972 that the Navy was considering recommissioning *New Jersey* to again deploy it to Vietnam, in fact the mighty battlewagon would remain laid up in reserve. At various times, military leaders advocated for returning one or more of the *Iowa*s, usually the *New Jersey*, to service for gunfire support, but none of those initiatives came to pass.

However, interest in reactivating the battleship was renewed in the late 1970s, although being opposed by President Carter and many within the Navy. Although gaining momentum, legislative leaders continued to debate the merits.

President Reagan, on the other hand, favored returning *New Jersey* and *Iowa* to service, as part of his campaign to build a 600-ship navy.

Arkansas senator Dale Bumpers vehemently opposed the reactivation of the battleships, at one point in the debate asking, "If 16-inch guns are so great, why have we not put one on a ship for the past thirty-five years?" His question found an unlikely respondent in the form of Jeremiah A. Denton Jr., senator from Alabama, retired naval aviator, and former prisoner of war, who had spent seven years as a POW. Denton calmly spoke, "I know the question from the senator is sincere, and I give him a sincere answer. In Vietnam, we lost hundreds of aircraft at a great cost in lives, as well as dollars, that could have been saved had a battleship been on station. A battleship could have knocked out the Thanh Hoa bridge that I was bombing at the time I was shot down. We lost five planes in one day on that one target. I point out that the Thanh Hoa bridge was only 12 miles inland, well within the range of the 16-inch guns on the *Iowa*-class battleships. There is a reason for those ships, and thank God the Navy is coming forward asking for them again." Beyond the purely strategic assets of the massive ships, which would be upgraded with new generations of weapons, including Harpoon and Tomahawk missiles augmenting their giant 16-inch rifles, there was a deterrent effect as well. Gen. Robert H. Barrow, commandant of the Marine Corps, explained it in simple terms, "You get a tremendous psychological effect from a battleship wherever it goes. People quickly realize this is something they can't deal with. North Vietnamese foot soldiers stood their ground and fired their rifles at supersonic jet airplanes, but nobody ever stood up to the *New Jersey*."

While initially consideration was given to removing the aft 16-inch turret to make way either for additional aircraft capacity or a vertical-launch missile system, those plans were soon abandoned. This change of plan, plus the prior removal of the light antiaircraft battery, greatly simplified the actual work of modernization. However, there was still considerable work to be done, notably in the removal of two 5-inch gun mounts on each side in order to make room for armored box launchers for Tomahawk cruise missiles, as well as the addition of Harpoon missile launchers and Phalanx Close-In Weapons Systems. The battleship would get a significant upgrade in its electronics suite, and, significantly for the crew, the ship was to be air conditioned.

On July 27, 1981, *New Jersey* began the long tow from Puget Sound to Long Beach for overhaul at the shipyard. After months of work, on September 25, 1982, *New Jersey* set out for sea trials. Finally, on 28 December the ship was recommissioned, with President Ronald Reagan as the keynote speaker during the ceremonies.

Following extensive training and "showing the flag" cruises, in September 1983 *New Jersey* was ordered to a position off the coast of Lebanon, which was in the grips of a civil war. A multinational force of peacekeepers were attempting to restore order, and in April the US embassy there had been bombed, killing sixty-three. In August, US Marines, a part of the peacekeeping force, came under fire, and the Reagan administration thought that the *New Jersey* could provide the support the Marines needed. Indeed, a ceasefire was declared the day *New Jersey* took position off Beirut. In the words of USMC Gen. P. X. Kelly, "There is no weapon system in the world that comes even close to the visible symbol of enormous power represented by the battleship."

The ceasefire did not last long, and in October a truck bomb killed 241 peacekeepers in a barracks. The result was that the *New Jersey* was ordered to remain on station, and its crew rotated for relief. On December 14, 1983, it fired its first 16-inch rounds in anger since 1969, striking Syrian/Druze antiaircraft batteries. *New Jersey* continued to provide fire support intermittently into 1984. During this time it was learned that there was considerable inaccuracy of the guns, which was traced to a poor remixing of powder by the Naval Weapons Center, Crane, Indiana.

In 1986, *New Jersey* began operating with the Pacific Fleet, where it remained until again decommissioned for budgetary reasons on February 8, 1991, as its sister ships *Wisconsin* and *Missouri* took part in Operation Desert Storm.

On July 27, 1981, tugboats are moving the battleship *New Jersey* from its berth at the Puget Sound Naval Shipyard, preparatory to towing it to Long Beach, California, for modernization and reactivation. The tugboat with its bow pressing against *New Jersey*'s bow is the civilian boat *Shelly Foss*. Alongside *New Jersey*'s port beam is the fleet tug USS *Takelma* (ATF-113). Note the notch cut into the bulwark on the forecastle, to accommodate storing the anchor in that position. This was done to free up the port hawse pipe so a tow cable could be routed through it. (The starboard anchor had already been dismounted, so its hawse pipe was available for a tow cable.) *US Navy*

The *New Jersey* is viewed from astern in dry dock at Long Beach in December 1981. Whereas the 1967–68 reactivation of this battleship had cost $23 million, the 1981–82 refitting was much more extensive and had a price tag of $326 million. *US Navy*

The battleship *New Jersey* is viewed from above as it is being towed from Bremerton to Long Beach on August 2, 1981. The voyage under tow extended along virtually the entire West Coast of the lower-48 United States. The ship reached Long Beach on August 6, and it was docked alongside Pier Echo. *US Navy*

The ship is observed from off its port bow in dry dock in February 1982. The ECM compartment on the forward fire-control tower that was built on during the 1967–68 modernization has by now been replaced by an entirely new structure, below the forward Mk. 38 main-battery director. Scaffolding surrounds the forward fire-control tower. *US Navy*

The forward fire-control tower and the front of the superstructure, encased in scaffolding, as well as part of turret 2, are viewed close-up in this February 1982 photograph. *US Navy*

In February 1982, the *New Jersey* is viewed off its starboard bow in dry dock at Long Beach. The notch in the bulwark on its forecastle has been plugged, and a major remodeling is underway to its forward fire-control tower. The hull had been repainted since the ship entered dry dock, but the boot topping remains to be applied along the waterline. *US Navy*

In a view from astern in dry dock, the aircraft crane on the fantail has been removed permanently, as part of a project to enlarge the helipad and its facilities. The two gun tubs on the stern will remain but will be put to other uses, for helicopter support. The port tub would become a helicopter fueling station. Farther forward, a trailer parked across the deck serves as an engineer's office. *US Navy*

Workmen are boarding the *New Jersey* in dry dock at Long Beach during February 1982. In the foreground is turret 3. During this modernization, four of the ten twin 5-inch/38-caliber gun mounts were removed to provide space for a new missile deck between the smokestacks. *US Navy*

By late summer 1982, the refitting of the *New Jersey* was complete. It is seen here navigating rough water during its first round of sea trials off the Pacific coast on September 25, 1982. The ship had a new, tripod foremast, with SPS-49 air-search radar on top. The object shaped like a crane alongside the aft part of the superstructure is a newly installed underway replenishment (UNREP) kingpost, also sometimes referred to as the refueling-at-sea (RAS) kingpost, used in managing fuel lines when refueling escorting ships while underway. *US Navy*

A crewman is operating the throttle for one of the engines of the *New Jersey* during sea trials in September 1982. A comparison of this photo with the April 1953 photo of the throttle wheel and instrument panel in Engine Room No. 3 on page 68 reveals that little had changed in the layout of gauges and controls in the intervening twenty-nine years. *US Navy*

In a photograph taken from the fantail of the *New Jersey*, the crew is manning the rails as the ship prepares to depart for sea trials prior to its recommissioning. Note the tarpaulins lashed over the former gun tubs in the foreground. The distinctive form of the UNREP kingpost is to the starboard beam of the superstructure. *US Navy*

Members of the crew of the *New Jersey* enjoy a meal during sea trials in September 1982. *US Navy*

Ammunition handlers are wheeling a pallet of ammunition for the 16-inch guns along the main deck of the battleship *New Jersey* during preparations for its reactivation, in October 1982. *US Navy*

Crewmen on the main deck are unloading a rack of ammunition during preparations for the second round of sea trials in October 1982. In the right background are two of the twin 5-inch/38-caliber gun mounts. *US Navy*

The *New Jersey* cruises off the California coast, inbound to Long Beach Naval Shipyard during its second round of sea trials in October 1982. This round of sea trials lasted four days. During this foray, the ship's new Vulcan/Phalanx 20 mm Close-In Weapon System (CIWS; pronounced "see-wiz") was fired for the first time, and the guns of the main and secondary batteries also were test-fired. *US Navy*

The right gun of turret 1 is firing during weapons tests on October 20, 1982. Secretary of the Navy John Lehman was aboard to witness this series of weapons tests. *US Navy*

The left gun of turret 2 has just fired a round during a test of the *New Jersey*'s weapons systems off the coast of California on October 20, 1982. That gun was set at a high angle of elevation when fired. *US Navy*

Military and civilian spectators in the grandstand in the foreground are present for the recommissioning ceremony for the *New Jersey* on December 28, 1982. The ship was prepared for modern warfare, being armed, in addition to its 16-inch and 5-inch batteries, with eight armored box launcher (ABL) mounts for 32 BGM-109 Tomahawk cruise missiles, 16 RGM-84 Harpoon antiship missiles, and four Phalanx CIWS antimissile and antiaircraft guns. *US Navy*

President Ronald Reagan was the honored speaker at the recommissioning of USS *New Jersey* at Long Beach on December 28, 1982. *US Navy*

Crewmen are marching toward the gangway to board the *New Jersey* during its recommissioning ceremony. President Reagan and other dignitaries are seated behind the bunting on the 01 level, alongside the aft part of turret 2. *US Navy*

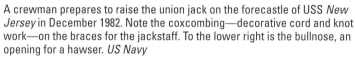

A crewman prepares to raise the union jack on the forecastle of USS *New Jersey* in December 1982. Note the coxcombing—decorative cord and knot work—on the braces for the jackstaff. To the lower right is the bullnose, an opening for a hawser. *US Navy*

Bunting is rigged to the rails along the main deck of USS *New Jersey* during its recommissioning ceremony on December 28, 1982. Towering above the foretop is a topmast that was installed during the 1981–82 modernization. This mast contained TACAN and omnidirectional VHF and UHF antennas, lights, a homing beacon, and a lightning rod on top. *US Navy*

An RGM-84 Harpoon antiship missile has just been launched from USS *New Jersey* during an exercise at the Pacific Missile Test Center Range on March 23, 1983. The launchers for the Harpoon missiles are abeam the aft smokestack. Originally developed and built by McDonnell Douglas, the Harpoon is an all-weather, over-the-horizon antiship missile with active radar homing and very low-level trajectory. *US Navy*

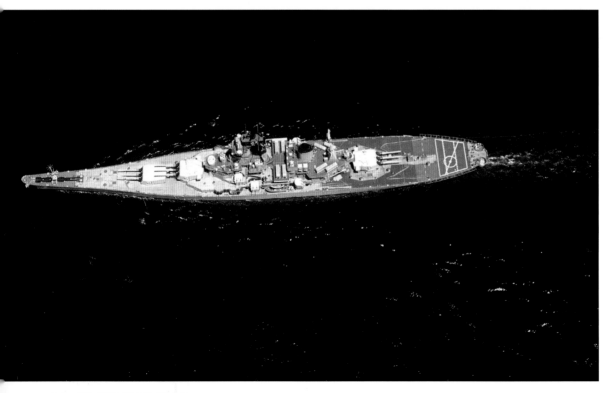

USS *New Jersey* is viewed from above and slightly to port in the Pacific during April 1983. The armored box launchers for the BGM-109 Tomahawk cruise missiles are visible, arranged diagonally on the level aft of the aft smokestack, and laterally on the level between the two smokestacks. Safety nets are now present alongside the helipad. *US Navy*

Along with other ships of a task group, USS *New Jersey* operates off the California coast on April 15, 1983. The feature on the center of the stern is the ports for the AN/SLQ-25 anti-torpedo system. *US Navy*

A Tomahawk missile has just been launched from an ABL on USS *New Jersey* during a test firing off the coast of Southern California in May 1983. The trajectory of the Tomahawk would take it nearly 500 miles to its target at the Tonopah Test Range, Nevada. Note the Phalanx CIWS with its white radome to the right of the photo. *US Navy*

Surrounded by starlets, Bob Hope entertains the crew of USS *New Jersey* while operating in waters off Beirut, Lebanon, on Christmas Eve 1983. The ladies are (*left to right*) Judy Hyek, Miss USA; Cathy Lee Crosby; Ann Jillian; and Brooke Shields. The ship was stationed off Beirut to provide security for US Marines ashore. *US Navy*

Entering full production in 1978, the General Dynamics Phalanx CIWS is a highly accurate, radar-directed, fully automated M61 Vulcan 20 mm Gatling gun. As a self-contained weapon system, the Phalanx could acquire and track incoming targets and direct the Vulcan gun. The Phalanx replaced the old 40 mm and 20 mm antiaircraft batteries and served as the last line of defense against antiship missiles and aircraft attacking at close range. All four Phalanx CIWS mounts on USS *New Jersey* were on the 05 level: two to the immediate front of the forward fire-control tower, and two immediately forward of the aft smokestack. *US Navy*

In May 1984, Disney characters lead a procession up a gangway to the USS *New Jersey* to welcome members of the crew back to the ship's home port of Long Beach, California, after eleven months at sea. During that time, the *New Jersey* had operated with the Pacific Fleet and in the Mediterranean. *US Navy*

Beginning in June 1984, the *New Jersey* began a period of extensive refitting at Long Beach Naval Shipyard. It is seen here in dry dock during that overhaul, with the starboard rudder and propellers in the foreground. Heavy corrosion is visible on the propeller blades and the adjacent hull. *US Navy*

A view forward from the forward fire-control tower of the *New Jersey* provides details of the forward Mk. 37 secondary-battery director, the top of the conning tower, the twin 35-foot whip antennas, and the roofs of turrets 1 and 2. *US Navy*

A CH-46D Sea Knight helicopter is about to touch down on the helipad on the fantail of USS *New Jersey* in February 1985. Aft of turret 3, sailors in red helmets and jerseys are lined up behind a deck house; this structure served as the aviation services center. On the roof of the structure is a 15-foot trussed whip antenna. *US Navy*

Members of the crew of USS *New Jersey* are in dress whites and are manning the rails as the ship prepares to enter Pearl Harbor on May 24, 1986. Beginning that spring, the *New Jersey* was the lead ship of its own battle group, the first time this had occurred since the Korean Conflict. This group was named Battle Group Romeo. *US Navy*

In the area aft of turret 3, crewmen of the *New Jersey* are being treated to a cookout during March 1987. Occasional cookouts were a good morale builder, and a chance for personnel to enjoy a meal outside the confines of the mess areas in the ship. *US Navy*

New Jersey's crew mans the rails as the battleship steams up the entrance channel to Pearl Harbor. During this cruise, the ship would operate from Southeast Asia north to the Bering Sea. *US Navy*

USS *New Jersey* cruises along Cockburn Sound, in the outer port of Fremantle, Western Australia, on September 3, 1988. The ship was visiting the port for refueling, and it was the first battleship ever to enter Cockburn Sound. Note the safety net along the helipad in its raised position. The net could be lowered when helicopters were landing or taking off from the pad. *US Navy*

Photographers and film crews are braving the blast effect as the 16-inch/50-caliber guns of USS *New Jersey* fire a broadside salvo to open the celebration of the Australian bicentennial in October 1988. This occurred during a Western Pacific deployment of the battleship. *US Navy*

Smoke billows from a target ship as shells from USS *New Jersey* and USS *Missouri* detonate on it during Fleet Exercise '89 in the Pacific in October 1989. *US Navy*

Following the fall of the Soviet Union and resulting cuts to the US defense budget, USS *New Jersey* was decommissioned for the fourth and final time on February 8, 1991, and was placed in reserve at the Ship Intermediate Maintenance Facility, Puget Sound Naval Shipyard. The *New Jersey* is seen in this aerial view in May 1993, with seven decommissioned frigates of the *Knox* class nested alongside her. *US Navy*

CHAPTER 6
Museum Status

Following decommissioning in Long Beach, *New Jersey* was towed to Bremerton and returned to the reserve fleet. On February 12, 1995, *New Jersey* (and the rest of the *Iowa*s) was stricken from the Naval Vessel Register, indicating that it was no longer considered a military asset and would no longer be maintained as such. The training mechanisms of *New Jersey*'s main battery turrets were welded in place, in a move considered to be intended to ensure that the ship could not be returned to service. Congress objected to the disposal of the ships by the Navy, and the National Defense Authorization Act of 1996 ordered the Navy to reinstate two of the battleships as mobilization assets. Since the donation process for *Missouri* was well progressed, and *Iowa* had unrepaired blast damage in turret 2, *New Jersey* and *Wisconsin* were selected to be reinstated. The reprieve was short lived, since the Strom Thurmond National Defense Authorization Act of 1999 required that the Navy instead list and maintain the *Iowa* and *Wisconsin*, and also required that *New Jersey* be donated to a not-for-profit within the state of New Jersey for use as a memorial within the state. The change of status occurred in January 1999, and in September of that year *New Jersey* was towed from Bremerton to Philadelphia. There the ship was reconditioned for use as a museum, even though at that time no site or custodian had been selected. Ultimately, the decision was made to award the ship to the Home Port Alliance group and place it on the Camden, New Jersey, waterfront. There it remains as a museum and memorial.

Since 2000, the battleship *New Jersey* has been preserved as a museum ship on the waterfront at Camden, New Jersey. This series of walk-around photos of the ship was taken during 2008. It is seen here off its starboard bow. Awnings are rigged alongside turrets 1 and 2 and above the fantail. *David Doyle*

The foredeck of the *New Jersey* is observed from between the anchor chains. On a tubular frame straddling the deck is the antenna array for the Naval Tactical Data System (NTDS). *David Doyle*

Turrets 1 and 2 and the front of the superstructure of the *New Jersey* are viewed from the foredeck. Teak decks are always subject to decay, and the one in the foreground is no exception. Below the 16-inch/50-caliber guns of turret 1 is the steel breakwater. Four ladders are on the front of each turret, for accessing the turret roof. *David Doyle*

The roofs of turrets 2 (foreground) and 1 are viewed through the windscreen of the enclosed navigating bridge. At the bottom of the photo are the two periscope heads for the turret officer's booth. On the turret 2 roof are various brackets and a collapsible tripod for use in highline transfer operations. *David Doyle*

In a view of the starboard side of the *New Jersey* amidships, at the center of the photo is a boat davit, installed as part of the 1981–82 modernization of the ship. Under the davit, a motor whaleboat is stored above a captain's gig. To the upper left are four launcher tubes for RGM-84 Harpoon antiship missiles, with red covers over the fronts. *David Doyle*

The *New Jersey*'s underway replenishment (UNREP) kingpost, installed in 1981–82, is viewed from aft, along the rear of the starboard side of the superstructure. Above the superstructure are the aft fire-control tower, topped by the aft Mk. 38 director with the Mk. 13 radar antenna mounted above it, and the aft smokestack. Above the UNREP kingpost is the foremast. *David Doyle*

The UNREP kingpost and the aft part of the superstructure are viewed from a more forward perspective. An "E" signifying an award for excellence in the engineering department is marked in red on the aft smokestack. Abeam the aft smokestack are a pair of four-tube Harpoon missile launchers, below which is a twin 5-inch/38-caliber gun mount. *David Doyle*

In a view from the fantail, in the foreground at the bottom is the rear face of the aviation services center, with three hooded lights on the rear of the roof and a 15-foot trussed 10–30 megahertz antenna on the roof. On the rear of the superstructure just above the top of turret 3, the compartment with the square windows is the helicopter control station. *David Doyle*

Situated on a platform between the two smokestacks are the two forward armored box launcher (ABL) mounts for the BGM-109 Tomahawk cruise missiles. The view is from the starboard side of the platform. The front launcher is in the firing position, with a dummy warhead shown bursting through the tube cover, in a simulated launching. *David Doyle*